I Would Die for You

One Student's Story of Passion, Service, and Faith

Brent and Deanna Higgins

with excerpts from the writings of BJ Higgins

Revell

Grand Rapids, Michigan

© 2008 by Brent and Deanna Higgins

Published by Revell
a division of Baker Publishing Group
P.O. Box 6287, Grand Rapids, MI 49516-6287

Third printing, August 2008

Printed in the United States of America

Library of Congress Cataloging-in-Publication Data
Higgins, Brent.
    I would die for you : one student's story of passion, service, and faith / Brent and Deanna Higgins ; with excerpts from the writings of BJ Higgins.
        p.   cm.
    ISBN 978-0-8007-3244-8 (pbk.)
    1. Higgins, B. J. 2. Christian teenagers—United States—Biography. I. Higgins, Deanna. II. Higgins, B. J. III. Title.
    BR1725.H463H54 2008
    277.3'083092—dc22   2007036663

Published in association with Yates & Yates, LLP, Attorneys and Counselors, Orange, California.

Contents

Contents

Preface

BJ's room. We sit, side by side, on the carpet next to his narrow bed. These days we end up here more often than not. We sense a Presence—and we're not the only ones who notice it.

Yes, it looks like a young man's room. There on the dresser rests, as he put it, the "wicked awesome" stereo we gave him for his fifteenth birthday. His collection of root beer bottles lines the windowsill. His shoes lie, neatly arranged, on a low shelf in the closet—all of them, that is, except the brown clogs that Mom likes to slip on sometimes. It's one more small way of connecting with our son.

Posters cover the walls. We never paid much attention to how many he had. Now the number seems amazing, especially since nearly all of them exalt Christ or point to others (like MercyMe) who do.

The posters share space with other things BJ found important: two maps of Peru; his beloved bass guitar, gleaming red and white; an Inca Kola sticker; notes and pictures from friends; a Lord of the Rings calendar, still turned to August 2005, when his illness suddenly accelerated.

As we left for the hospital that day, did he know he would never return to this room? Not long before, he had spent time cleaning it up without our urging—not a normal activity for a fifteen-year-old. Did he have a clue that someday others would look into his room—his life?

When friends and family enter, they encounter something significant. To some, the experience brings closure. To others, laughter, as events and conversations come back to mind. Still others discover tears where they did not expect to find them. Many more remove their shoes, ending up on their faces before the Lord. Tears come again as they inhale both the presence of God and the memories of a young man so committed to Christ.

As we invite you into this paper-and-ink expression of BJ's life, we invite you to a similar experience. Sit on the carpet beside us. Look through his writings, his pictures, the words that family and friends share. Make yourself comfortable—and then allow the Spirit of God to make you just the opposite.

Holy ground does not allow long seasons of rest. God's purposes for your life include the truths expressed in these pages. Read, learn of him, and prepare to take your place in raising a revolution.

Join us as we share BJ's legacy and exalt the One he served with his whole heart. Jesus, we love you!

Dad and Mom

(Brent and Deanna Higgins)

The New Patient

I remember our intensivist, Dr. Williams, getting the call about BJ from a physician at another hospital. I was in charge that day and would be admitting this teenager, who was coming in via ambulance with a diagnosis of respiratory distress. All I could deduce about him at this time was that he was well enough to come by regular ambulance and that he probably had some type of pneumonia. I got room 5 in the corner all ready for him.

As he rolled through the unit late in the afternoon with the ambulance crew, all I could see was a thin boy with a mass of dark brown hair, lying on the stretcher with an oxygen mask over his face. He assisted us in getting him into the regular bed, and the ambulance team left after leaving his X-ray and hospital papers with us. I began hooking him up to our cardiac monitors and we started to chat—actually, *he* started to chat! It was then that I had the awesome opportunity to have an hour or so before the end of my shift to talk to BJ before his ordeal of overwhelming illness began. I introduced myself and began to tell him about all of the stuff we were going to have to do: monitors, labs, X-rays, and so on.

Most kids his age would just grunt as you relayed this information. Not BJ! He was full of questions, comments, and more questions. At one point he was trying to catch his breath midsentence while hypothesizing how the oximeter probe on his toe actually measured the oxygen in his blood. I remember telling him to "save his breath for breathing." He managed to tell me, between gulps of the sweet, 100 percent–saturated oxygen flowing through his mask, about his recent trip to Peru. Very early in our conversation, he asked me if I was a Christian. I said yes, I was.

I was taken aback by the boldness of this boy with the messy hair and the dirty white sport socks. I sensed then that this was not just an ordinary teenager but an amazing young man, much wiser than his years on this earth. Our conversation took place as I was scurrying about doing the many things that needed to be done for one of the very sickest patients I would ever take care of.

DONNA GUIDER, RN
ST. VINCENT'S HOSPITAL, INDIANAPOLIS, INDIANA

The Basics

How can a young man keep his way pure?
By living according to your word.

PSALM 119:9 (NIV)

one

Love Is a Verb

Love is not just an emotion, as the world sees it. It is action. While admittedly it does have emotion involved with it, it is not as unstable or changeable as emotions are. Affections come and go, grow and fade, but love does not. It is constant because it is more than an emotion; it is more of a constant state of selflessness that produces action.

BJ HIGGINS
FROM A LETTER TO A FRIEND • 2004

Love. Just do it.

Love. The word screams at you from the car stereo speakers booming their way through the traffic. It whispers from the ads spinning through cyberspace and appearing on your computer screen. You may even find it wrapped around the brightly colored cups at the fast-food counter or highlighting the menu when

11

you stop for a Starbucks. Friends toss it off so easily: "I *love* your hair!" "He *loves* seafood." "Didn't you *love* him in that movie?"

Love meant much more than an offhand comment or casual phrase to BJ Higgins. In his words, love was not just what you said—but what you *did*.

Love. BJ taught it. He lived it. He died for it.

This is his story.

Love at first sight? We (Brent and Deanna—BJ's friends and others from his generation call us Mom and Dad, so that's how we'll refer to ourselves in this book) still disagree about that. It happened in Houston, Texas. Although we had seen one another off and on, the Indiana boy and the petite Southern girl did not officially meet until the middle of the summer of 1982, when we attended the same class at church. Mom had recently graduated from Houston Baptist University, and Dad was a fresh transplant to Houston after finishing college in his home state of Indiana.

> [Seeing her for the first time] caused my jaw to spontaneously free-fall to its fullest open position. I immediately bowed my head, and said, "Father, if there is any way, this is the girl I want to marry!"
>
> Dad, blog posting
> January 14, 2006

We shared similar backgrounds: a deep faith, close family relationships, a strong interest in music. Attraction moved rapidly into a love that quickly drew us to marriage. Within just a few months, Brent Allen Higgins and Deanna Louise Tucker were wed at her brother Dan's home in nearby Deer Park.

Love (and Dad's desire to beat the heat) drew us to new jobs and a new home in the Indianapolis area. The arrival of first one, then another baby girl (Lauren Breanne and Whitney Louise) multiplied the love. It also changed the location of "home" from a tiny apartment to a larger duplex to a three-bedroom house.

This home, and this family, welcomed Brent Allen Higgins Jr. (we usually called him "BJ") to the world on October 1, 1989.

BJ, Lauren, and Whitney

There was a mild element of disappointment when the ultrasound showed he was a girl—after two girls, we were really hoping for a boy. I think Deanna was more disappointed than I was. When he was born, the doctor said, "You have a son." I couldn't believe what I was hearing! I remember immediately picking up the phone and calling my father. This was his first grandson.

Dad

BJ loved to hear the story of the ultrasound that incorrectly identified him as a girl and his astonished family's delight in his birth. Later, he described their response:

My grandfather was not the only family member that was excited. Almost everyone was, but my sisters were especially. They didn't really care at the time if I was a girl or a boy; they were just happy that I was a baby. I have two sisters, both older than me, and I was my parents' first son. When I was born, my sister Whitney was two years old, and my sister Lauren was four years old. Though some people thought my sisters would be jealous of me and of the attention I received; on the contrary, they were thrilled at my arrival! They sometimes even fought over who could hold me next.

From "BJ Higgins" • 2003

The self-assurance that led BJ to write those words in his autobiography "BJ Higgins" (a school assignment) flowed naturally from our family atmosphere. In a world of broken families and painful relationships, BJ knew something radically different. He knew love as much more than a casual phrase. To our son, love was always an action—a lifestyle—a legacy.

> BJ was always very loving. All our kids were very affectionate. I had people telling me that when the second and third ones came along, the older ones might be jealous, but that never happened. When BJ was born, the girls both thought he was their baby. They were so affectionate, and I was very thankful for that.
>
> Mom

Spend time with the Higgins/Tucker extended family and you'll experience this love full force. Our eyes brighten and our voices warm when we talk about our children. Pore over the pages of one of Mom's scrapbooks and see the time, care, and love invested. Creativity and pictures matter. Lives matter even more.

Visit a family event to discover the same love in all directions. Cousins tumble over one another in their eagerness to reach an arriving uncle. Brothers and sisters, grown or not-yet-grown, take obvious delight in spending time together. Tickles, giggles, and hugs abound.

Frustrations, faults? Absolutely! Don't look for perfection—you won't find it. Instead, you'll see real people, real relationships—overflowing with acceptance, encouragement, laughter, and love.

From the moment of his birth, BJ Higgins began learning and living this life of love. Later, he described it as a family distinctive:

My family has always been very close, even close enough to know exactly how other family members will respond to certain things. It's instances like this that make me realize how fortunate I am to live in such a loving, caring family that isn't split up from divorce or separation, and isn't distant. So many people today are faced with the heart-wrenching trials of divorce or distance. Even when some families are close geographically, they are still very distant because of parted ways through disagreements or conflicting beliefs, disownment, or even just lack of communication. However, my family loves each other tremendously, even if we don't always get along.

www.xanga.com/DeadSilence7 • April 6, 2004

We have a close extended family, unusually close. We were blessed to be brought up that way.

Lauren Higgins

BJ used to lean on us. He was very affectionate and for that, I've always been grateful. . . . I'd be standing somewhere minding my own business and he would come up and start leaning. . . . It made me smile and now it reminds me of his love for me. I savor the memory. . . . What joy that boy gave!

Mom, blog posting
March 10, 2006

BJ spoke often about the love he experienced at the heart of his family, the source of his trademark tone of deep passion. Even as a young boy, he knew that love was more than just an idea.

I was reminded this past weekend of a conversation I had with BJ about six years ago. I don't remember why we started talking about love, but for some reason we did. We got into a very heated argument because BJ was trying to explain to me that love is a verb and I, being older, could

BJ leaning on his dad
(ski weekend)

not accept that I was wrong and so fought him, [insisting] that love is simply an idea. . . . In a recent Bible study, our college group came to the conclusion that faith is not an idea; it's a verb.

Just like love. Just like my little brother tried to tell me so many years ago. . . . Faith and love are part of a lifestyle, not a religion, and it's our job to show that to the world.

WHITNEY HIGGINS, BLOG POSTING • APRIL 19, 2006

It seems obvious that, even in his infancy, God had begun to prepare BJ for greatness—and that he was already a target of the Enemy. In his second week of life, BJ suffered a bout of pneumonia that landed him back in the hospital. Just a few months later, after he had begun to crawl, Dad found him flipped over on the carpet, blue and breathless. Scooping up his baby boy, he begged God to spare his life. A frantic finger sweep dislodged the culprit—a tiny piece of plastic. Once again the Lord rescued one who would grow to love and serve him in amazing ways.

BJ's friends and family all agree that when BJ talked, he often spoke beyond the moment. His words seemed to send echoes deep into eternity. His many writings, from childish journals to Internet postings, reveal this quality over and over again.

No doubt, the truths BJ absorbed from his earliest days shaped the following email.

1 Corinthians 13:4–7. Now that we have established that love is action, let's go back to 1 Corinthians 13. This passage states seven things that love is . . .

First, Love is patient. So often, we become very impatient and think little to nothing of it. . . . When we would find it easy to become impatient with someone, we should instead be patient, for love is patient, and Christ commanded that we love each other. . . .

16

Second, Love is kind. . . . *Remember every now and then when someone says something like "I love you in the God way" or "Well, I love them in the God way, but does that mean I have to be nice to them/you"? Riiiight, and please show me the love of God that doesn't require kindness. And remember, God not only commanded us to love our friends and family, but to love our enemies (Matthew 5:44). . . .*

The third thing love is/does, Love rejoices with the truth. . . . *it's pretty self-explanatory: love takes joy in the truth. It seeks it, not just for itself and of things, but it also seeks the truth of others.*

Next, Love bears all. *Love protects. Love has a big shoulder to take the hit for others. Love bears others' pain with them and for them. Love sympathizes and goes through ALL hard times with others and helps them through it. Notice that it says love bears ALL things. Not just sometimes, not just when the sun is shining, but ALLways. Love is there for you.*

Love believes all. *Love is positive about others. . . . We must, as it says, "Rejoice in the truth," and not hide from it, but we must be positive, especially when the truth is not known.*

Love hopes all. *This probably relates most to "Love is not jealous." Love hopes the best for others. . . . Love wants others to do well, to be in God's will. An action that expresses this is praying. When you pray for someone, you are displaying to God that you have love for him or her.*

And finally, Love endures all. *This one is HUGE. It is basically a summary of everything. If you get this, the others will happen. Consequently, it is the hardest to do. Love puts up with everything. . . .*

The Greek word used here is hupono, *which is a military term that means "above all else," or "no matter what the cost." If an army is going into battle, the captain might say, "Hold the fort* hupono!*"*

It is helpful, especially with a friend you spend a lot of time with, if they're a Christian, that they understand these points so that you can hold each other accountable when you start to slip up in a conversation by saying, "No, love endures all" or "Love bears all" or "Remember, love believes all."

Otherwise, remind yourself. Keep these verses on your heart.

FROM A LETTER TO A FRIEND • 2004

two

Divine Encounter

How to get to heaven is an issue often disagreed on, but the fact that some people don't believe the truth doesn't make it less true. I am here merely to offer you the truth. . . . Jesus came to earth only to die for the wrongdoings of others. And even though this perfect and holy Savior, the Messiah of the Jews, never sinned, he died to cleanse the sins of everyone who might put their faith in him. *"Jesus said, 'I am the way, the truth, and the life. No man comes to the Father except through me'"* (John 14:6).

BJ Higgins

"How to Get to Heaven: A Writing to Inform Paper on Salvation"

school assignment • 2003

Know Jesus.

Certainly, love surrounded BJ from his earliest days. So did Someone else. God was already at work, drawing BJ toward himself.

An insightful BJ later recognized this. He wrote:

19

All of my relatives value each other as much, if not more, as they value themselves. However, those of us who are old enough to understand put God before our family and ourselves. This is why I think that we have made it so far without being disconnected. . . . We have all been raised in a family who loves us and teaches us to put God above all other things, even ourselves.

FROM "BJ HIGGINS" • 2003

From infancy, BJ had learned to put God first. In our family's life, church involvement was already a given. Our own congregation, Northside Baptist, enthusiastically welcomed the newest little Higgins. BJ became especially well known there after he portrayed a very special baby in the church's 1989 Christmas production alongside our roles as Mary and Joseph.

> That year, I had put together a brief Christmas pageant. I asked Brent and Deanna to play Joseph and Mary. We did a living room set with Grandfather reading the Christmas story to the family. One of the little girls . . . was looking out of the window. While she did that, Mary and Joseph came down the aisle. They were on one side of the stage, reenacting the Christmas story, and BJ was obviously baby Jesus. . . . That was my first real memory of BJ.
>
> RUSTY KENNEDY, ASSOCIATE PASTOR AND MINISTER TO STUDENTS, NORTHSIDE BAPTIST CHURCH

Mom began teaching music at Tabernacle Christian Academy when BJ was three years old, and he attended preschool through first grade there. He recalled these years as "enjoyable, carefree times." We love to recall the many Bible verses he learned even at this young age. In fact, we believe that this early emphasis helped lay a solid foundation for a faith that grew fast and stayed strong.

A sudden loss shook that foundation, however. When BJ was only four years old, his Grandpa Higgins became very ill. He and BJ had always enjoyed an especially close bond.

> I remember him playing role reversal games with my husband. He would want to play Grandpa and want Grandpa to play BJ. They would sit for hours in the car playing that game. We would go and babysit them sometimes when Brent and Deanna were gone. Often they were not even excited to have their parents come home, because they would want us to stay longer!
>
> GRAMMA ETHEL HIGGINS

BJ (4 years old) and Grandpa straightening their ties

> *When he came over, we would play games like doctor, cars, and "Lincoln Logs." One thing that I especially remember and enjoyed is how we would switch places in the car, and I would "drive" him around for a while. Anytime we were together, fun was to be had.*
>
> *Unfortunately, one day even my amazing junior doctor skills couldn't fix his "fever." When I was four, he was diagnosed with cancer of the pancreas, and he was too far along even for surgery. . . . On August 26, 1994, around 8:00 p.m., while my sisters and I were at a friend of the family's house, he passed away.*
>
> FROM "BJ HIGGINS"

We all grieved deeply, but not "as others who have no hope" (1 Thess. 4:13). Still today family members point to Grandpa Higgins as a model of godly manhood. The time BJ spent with his grandfather shaped his life and solidified his firm foundation of faith. Again, God was at work to draw BJ toward the Savior he would come to know so well.

Sometimes, though, we build false fronts even over firm foundations. Later, BJ wrote:

About a year [after Grandpa's death], I felt left out in my family; they were all Christians, and I wasn't yet. So, one day in June 1995, I decided to become a Christian, even though I didn't really understand it. Pretending, I was baptized by one of my pastors.

FROM "BJ HIGGINS"

BJ had seen his older sisters accept Christ. It seemed only right that he ask Dad about it, and Dad explained how to receive Jesus as Savior, thinking his son understood. It seemed only right that baptism would follow. Two years later, at a youth meeting, BJ heard the salvation story again—from Afshin Ziafat, a man who had come to Christ from a Muslim background. This time, BJ "got it."

For the first time, he began to understand his spiritual lostness. That night at the invitation, he asked the Lord to save him. At first, we were confused—wasn't he already a Christian? Gradually, we came to understand what BJ already knew: this time was different. This time was *real.*

BJ's life changed after that night. His whole approach to his "walk" was filled with desire for knowledge and an understanding he did not previously have. He began sharing at school and with anyone who would listen. If an eight-year-old could be radically saved . . . he was.

Dad, blog posting
February 1, 2006

BJ laid out his new understanding of salvation in a journal entry written shortly after he accepted Christ:

Our relationship with God is from his grace = By God's grace we're saved. The faith we exercise is a gift from God's grace. . . . By Jesus' death, we're forgiven = By his blood our sins are washed away.

DECEMBER 9, 1998

About three years later at youth camp, BJ was rebaptized as a true believer in Christ. This time, he fully understood his commitment.

BJ getting baptized at youth camp

I remember baptizing him at camp. That was obviously a discussion we had. That's a fear we have as youth ministers, when a kid says, "I want to be rebaptized," especially at camp, is it really a spiritual marker, or is he doing it because it's a cool thing to do? I probably grilled him pretty hard, asking, "Why are you doing this?"

For BJ, it was because, one, it was a testimony; and, two, he wanted his friends to know for real that he had been saved. He wanted to tell the world that he loved Jesus and that his life had been changed.

PASTOR RUSTY KENNEDY

BJ wrote forcefully about his salvation experience in a school composition. Here he did something that had become his pattern—using a school assignment as a witnessing tool. In this paper, he wrote out the specific steps toward a saving relationship with Christ.

How to get to heaven is an issue often disagreed on, but the fact that some people don't believe the truth doesn't make it less true. I am here merely to offer you the truth on how to get to heaven. "God loved the world so much that he sacrificed his only Son so that whoever believes in him shall not die, but live on" (John 3:16). God's Son's name was Jesus, which means "Savior," or "God saves."

Jesus came to earth only to die for the wrongdoings of others. And even though this perfect and holy Savior, the Messiah of the Jews, never sinned, he died to cleanse the sins of everyone who might put their faith in him. "Jesus said, 'I am the way, the truth, and the life. No man comes to the Father except through me'" (John 14:6). When you believe that Jesus was the Messiah, that he died for your sins, and that he desires to know you and have a personal relationship with you, and when you confess your sins and commit your life to Jesus Christ, then you are saved from eternal damnation. "Jesus said to them, 'Whoever believes . . . will be saved, whoever does not believe will be condemned'" (Mark 16:16). A pastor once said that with Christ, you can have life, but without Christ, you merely exist. John 20:31c says "and by believing you can have life in his name."

Everyone on the face of this earth has sinned, but just as everyone has sinned, everyone can receive life. "For the cost of sin is death, but God's gift is eternal life in heaven" (Rom. 6:23). Only a person's faith in God can save him. "For it's by grace that you can be saved—through faith, and not of yourselves, but it's a gift from God" (Eph. 2:8). Even if you have very little faith, as long as you have faith, God will do the rest. "Even if you have faith in God the size of a mustard seed, nothing will be impossible for you" (Matt. 17:20). God says that you must believe in him, receive his word, confess your sins, and commit yourself to Christ to be saved. "If you confess with your mouth, 'Jesus is Lord,' and believe in your heart that God raised him from the dead, then you will be saved, for it is with your heart that you believe and are justified, and it is with your mouth that you confess and are saved" (Rom. 10:9–10). All you have to do to be saved and become a Christian is to simply do what I already said and just pray to God and ask Jesus Christ to come into your life and cleanse your sins.

From "How to Get to Heaven"

Someone else who would have rejoiced in BJ's newfound salvation was Mom's father, a longtime pastor. For years Papaw and Mamaw Tucker had encouraged BJ and their other grandchildren to walk with God. Every Christmas, when the entire family visited, Papaw arranged for his grandchildren to sing together at whichever church he was serving.

Only a month or so before BJ accepted Christ, Papaw had a terrible car accident. During his long recovery, seizures permanently damaged his brain. Since that time, Mamaw has tenderly cared for him in their Kentucky home.

I always knew that BJ was very, very deep spiritually, even as a little child. I remember when they visited, going in to tell them good night, and his daddy would have them down on their knees praying. They were just brought up that way—all three of these children were very deep spiritually. I remember BJ when he was just a tiny little thing, down on his knees by the bed. He was so precious. I knew he was very special.

Mamaw Louise Tucker

In 2003 BJ wrote a devotional for students to use at Northside's Ultimate Youth Camp. His words capture the faith he lived out:

25

*L*ove *the Lord your God with all your heart, with all your soul, and with all your mind" (Matt. 22:37). This is a familiar passage to many of us, but very few of us fully understand what it really means and can really carry this out. Christ said that we have to love him, and not just love him, but also to love him with everything that we are. So focus your mind on God, since it is now your nature, by turning to God for focus, because you are called to love him with your mind.*

Read Psalm 19:14. If your mind is thinking of bad things or reflecting on impure thoughts or ideas, is it really loving God? No, and since God deserves love, love him, and concentrate on him. Let the words that you say, the thoughts that you think, and the feelings of your heart glorify God. David was called a man after God's own heart, and I think that this passage shows why. Even though he didn't always do the right thing, and he often didn't, he had the desire to glorify God. Let this Scripture passage be your prayer and philosophy this week, and the rest of your life.

Pray that the Holy Spirit would turn your thoughts toward God and that God would give you a love for him beyond human comprehension. If you are not a Christian, and do not have a personal relationship with Jesus Christ, pray that the Holy Spirit would come into your life and control your mind and actions, and get to know your Savior by digging into the Word of God.

three

A Willing Witness

More long-term [among my goals], though, is that I hope to be an influencer at school, a light. If I help to show one person the way to God, if I can make one person question the meaning of life and find it, I will have fulfilled my goal and part of my purpose for living.

BJ HIGGINS • "GOALS" • SCHOOL ASSIGNMENT • FALL 2003

> Share the gospel.

As we like to say, "BJ got it." He understood salvation's true meaning. Immediately after receiving Christ as his Savior, he began sharing what he knew. Within a few months, he wrote:

Being in the right place at the right time can give you an opportunity. Paul and Silas were at the right place and at the right time, which led Lydia to Christ. That sent them to jail. At the jail Paul and Silas were in an earthquake that broke their chains and the jail keeper drew his sword and almost struck himself, but Paul said, "Don't, we're all here," and so the jail keeper asked, "Sirs, how must I be saved?" and he accepted Christ.

JOURNAL ENTRY • NOVEMBER 8, 1998

BJ believed in using the opportunities God gave him to share his faith with others. He also watched and listened with unusual understanding. Dad admits that when Lauren, Whitney, and BJ were young, his own faith was immature. He had the experience many parents have, watching the faults in his children's lives reflect weaknesses in his own. Gradually God began a work in his heart—one that would one day move him toward a call to ministry.

Deanna had been pouring herself out to the Lord, wanting me to be the spiritual leader of our home. At church I had taken on the role of deacon. Things looked good from the outside, but on the inside, I knew I did not have the kind of relationship with the Lord that I needed. BJ was watching me through that time. The Lord put his finger on my heart and said, "You need to change; you need to develop in some areas that you're not."

All through that period, Deanna was praying. I would pick up her Bible and it would make me feel sick inside—the way all the pages were marked up. I knew that the five minutes I spent with my Bible in the morning were not like that.

My call to ministry came from the hours Deanna spent seeking the Lord to change my life. When he did, I saw dramatic changes in BJ.

Dad

As Dad was growing spiritually, BJ was watching. Early in elementary school, he was watching when Dad told a neighbor boy how to have a relationship with Christ. He was watching when the boy received Jesus that same afternoon. Soon he began witnessing to friends on his own. His witness reached beyond his neighborhood to touch his classmates.

> It wasn't long after I had shared with the neighbor boy that BJ had a friend come into our home, again from our neighborhood. The boy was moving out of state the next day, and BJ, realizing that the young man wasn't a believer, wanted to share. He was very young, probably only second or third grade, but he started in Genesis and he went through the Bible, just talking to him about what the Bible meant and went all the way to Revelation, not necessarily stopping at every book but just vividly giving background and hitting the high points. I remember him saying very clearly, "Don't you want to have a relationship with Jesus?" and the young man said, "Yes, show me how!"
>
> And BJ told him how, and then he prayed with him, and it was amazing as a parent to see that kind of turnaround. I think when I started seeing changes reflected in BJ's life that God really started to use that. He used my youngest child to say, "What you see here in the mirror of your son's life—that's a reflection of who you are right now." God was changing me—and I immediately began to see the fruit of those changes in my son's life.
>
> Dad

BJ had a better grasp on spiritual things than I did at his age. There was no doubt in my mind that he took his relationship with the Lord very seriously at an early age, no doubt that he was doing things, reaching out to friends in a way that I never

BJ leading a boy to Jesus

did. I was very shy. I probably wouldn't even have gone next door to witness to a friend like he did when he was only seven or eight years old. There was always a depth there.

UNCLE BRAD HIGGINS

During BJ's early years of school, things did not always go well. After he finished first grade, Mom began teaching music in one public school, and BJ transferred to the one nearest his home, Oaklandon Elementary. His teachers pointed out that he struggled to maintain focus. Eventually, he was diagnosed with attention deficit disorder and began taking medication to help him concentrate. Later BJ described himself as "a mess" during that period. He hated taking the medication and rejoiced when, later in elementary school, he outgrew the problem.

I think that sometimes he felt overpowered by two older sisters and four people telling him what to do. There were times he felt pretty smothered by that, but I think in the long run, that was one of the things that made him so strong as a person. He learned to stand up for himself instead of keeping it inside, sharing it with me, or writing about it in his journal. He learned to speak out and be strong in that way, and it really helped him later.

GRAMMA ETHEL HIGGINS

BJ loved roughhousing with our boys. We would usually get together once or twice a year, and our boys, being older, would tire of it before BJ did. He was always riding on their shoulders. They all got along well.

Lauren, Whitney, and BJ in 2000

Any time that a comment came up about BJ not having a long attention span, our older son, David, would take up for him and say that he was a cool kid who just needed to be given a chance.

AUNT JOLENE TUCKER

Growing up as the youngest child and only boy in his family was a place of privilege—and challenge. Even in the midst of his struggles at school, BJ cared deeply about those around him.

Sometimes I feel as if I'm the only Christian. . . . This year I've seen a lot of immoral things from teachers and kids. That really disappoints me. The things disappoint me so much I feel like the world will collapse. It's so disgusting to see or think about what I've seen. I've never felt this way before and I feel so horrible I can't think about anything except this "spiritual struggle." I feel a burden to change these ways but I'm trying to find out how to do something about this sin.

JOURNAL ENTRY • DECEMBER 9, 1998

Once again BJ stood ready to put his beliefs into practice. His deep concern for others became a compelling drive to share the gospel. When he had missed an opportunity, he knew it—even as a third grader. He wrote about it in his journal:

I feel like I have failed with explaining your Word to my unsaved friends. I never understood the true meaning of when the thief accepted Christ. On his last chance and last moment of his life, he made his best decision of his life. I feel like I failed to tell my friend Kenny the Word of Jesus and help him understand what it means to accept Jesus as his Lord and Savior and give his life to him. Now Kenny's moved and I never took any opportunity that was given to me and now I regret it. It wasn't a good decision to make.

JOURNAL ENTRY • "FEELINGS" • MARCH 1999

31

I had BJ in third grade. He was a neat kid, just awesome. He brought his Bible to school every day. Any time that they finished their work, they had free reading time. BJ always got out his Bible—that's what he read. Even as a third grader, he was so much more mature than most kids. You knew the Lord had his hand on him.

LYNN DAILEY, FAMILY FRIEND AND THIRD-GRADE TEACHER

When BJ was in elementary school, he had just heard Afshin Ziafat speak and he accepted Christ. He wanted to be real. I remember hearing him at the bus stop, talking to a kid about the Lord. He was saying, "What if the bus crashes?" and asking if he knew Jesus. He was so young. It was obvious that there was a call on his life.

LAUREN • DECEMBER 30, 2005

Literally, from second grade on, if he had to talk about himself, if he had to stand in front of a group at school to give a speech, or if he had to write a paper, it was always about the Lord. He shared the gospel so many times every year in school—at recess but also during times of education. He was just witnessing.

Dad

One day I had a little boy come up to me. He was really upset. I said, "What's the matter?" Now, this was one of the little boys that rode BJ's bus every day, and he was crying and saying, "BJ told me if I don't ask Jesus in my heart, I'm going to hell." I had to talk to BJ too. I said, "What you told him is right, but let's see if we can tone it down a little, be kinder. Help him to understand the love of Jesus." BJ would always listen to whatever you had to say and take it seriously.

LYNN DAILEY

BJ had some growing to do. Still, he wrote what he lived and lived what he believed:

I know God can do radical things through children, and I don't mean to brag, but God has done radical things through my family. . . . now I'm in the third grade and nine years old.

Journal entry • December 9, 1998

As BJ matured and became more sensitive, his methods for sharing the gospel improved, and his passion deepened. That year, when the family moved to the Indianapolis suburb of Carmel, he began fifth grade in a new school. During this year, he played a lead role in the class production of *The Wizard of Oz*. BJ's size—always smaller than others his age—made the play's climax especially funny. Even his former teachers still remember the big voice coming from the tiny young man: "I am the great and powerful . . . Oz!"

BJ had changed schools—but not priorities.

Already I have many friends and feel as though I'm their best friend. But there's a greater reason I'm writing: "A school without Christianity is no place to learn." Unfortunately my school has very (very) little amount of people who are Christians. I only know of a couple people out of about 100 who are Christians. God has called me to witness to them (or some). I've tried to witness to three so far, but I'm still trying to tell them about salvation.

Journal entry • December 12, 2000

In sixth grade BJ began attending Clay Junior High as an honor student. Again, his school changed, but his commitment to witnessing stayed strong.

I remember Brent (BJ) from my sixth-grade English class at Clay. We had to write a paper on our best friends. His was about his accountability partner, and the close, like-a-brother relationship they had. This was the first example I had of how

33

deep relationships can go through Christ. Also, we had to write about our hero. Most people wrote about generic [people] like George Washington or one of their parents. Brent wrote about Jesus. I thought it was the coolest thing—that Jesus was actually his best friend.

BLOG POSTING • SEPTEMBER 27, 2005

I'm so amazed at the vivid memory I have of Brent [BJ used his given name, Brent, during elementary and middle school] from when we were seventh graders.... An assignment of ours was to complete a "book talk" on our favorite book. Brent did his report on the Left Behind series, and in doing so, shared the gospel to a group of seventh graders at Clay. I was a Christian at the time, but wasn't living it. I remember thinking, "Wow ... HE HAS WHAT I'M LOOKING FOR!! That is so cool he can be so bold." He's one of the first people that introduced me to a personal relationship with Christ, and I don't think he ever had any idea.

KARA PALMER, BLOG POSTING • SEPTEMBER 27, 2005

BJ's habit of leaving folded papers in his pockets often annoyed us—especially on laundry day. The following note (rescued before it hit the machines) was written in 2005. It shows the way our son's passion for Jesus turned even note-passing into a chance to share the gospel.

In getting to know me, the first and foremost thing you'll discover is that I am 100% a Jesus Freak. I have given my entire life to live for him. Whenever I am in a bad mood or if I have had a horrible day, I think of him and his love and companionship, and that always brings me joy.

More so than that, even, he gives my life purpose and meaning and fills that . . . emptiness inside of me that we all have that causes us to yearn for more, like money or a boyfriend or girlfriend or drugs or love, etc. And I have found that whereas all of these things may make you feel better for a moment, it will pass, and you will always want more.

However, basking in Jesus Christ's forgiveness and love is the only thing that will satisfy. So I want to encourage you: do not seek companionship from me or any other guy, but from the only one who can fill that void: the one who put it there, Jesus.

He will never let you down or not satisfy you like I or anyone else would.

In Christ's love,

BJ Higgins

P.S. By the way, it's very nice to meet you . . .

four

Passion for the Ultimate

I went to after school guys' Bible study, which definitely put me in a hopeless, lonely, cynical mood, because of the guys' hypocrisy; they put on these masks in church/Bible study and act like they're all good and straight, etc., then leave and cuss people out, caring less about God. Certainly I am not perfect and I am also hypocritical at times, [but] at least I try to obey God and my heart is one desiring for him. Anyway, it makes me feel like I am alone in my generation at my school in truly loving and striving to obey God; I feel like I am the only one with a true passion for the ultimate, my God.

BJ HIGGINS • WWW.XANGA.COM/DEADSILENCE7 • MARCH 8, 2004

Know the Word.

BJ loved God passionately. One of the ways he showed that passion best was his constant hunger for the Word of God. He loved reading, studying, and memorizing the Scriptures. If you could take a look at any of his several Bibles, you would see this clearly. He highlighted not just verses but entire sections, even in the Bibles he owned as a new Christian. Thinking back, we recall that his knowledge of the Word began very early in life.

> He had memorized lots of Scripture. I felt that going to the Christian preschool and kindergarten where his mother taught, that was a great asset to BJ in his early spiritual training. He memorized many Scriptures there. He learned to find them quickly and became very interested in the Scriptures at a very young age.
>
> GRAMMA ETHEL HIGGINS

> While still in preschool, he started memorizing Scripture, and when we visited my parents, one of the main things he liked to do on the drive was to say, "Mommy, Daddy, do you know this Scripture?" He would give us the address and want to know if we could recite the Scripture. Of course he knew all of them. That was another thing that was a little bit humbling, because he just knew so much Scripture!
>
> Dad

Some of his earliest journal entries, recorded in childlike printing, show the depth of his Bible study.

Psalm 14, verse 1: That man is a fool who says to himself, "There is no god." Anyone who talks like that is warped and evil and can't really be a good person at all. Verse 6: He is a refuge to the poor and humble when evildoers are oppressing them.

If one of your friends says, "God isn't real," don't just say, "You're a fool," correct them, explain why they are wrong (nicely), and say the verse Psalm 14:1–6. Also, say 1 Peter 3:4 which says,

"Be beautiful inside, in your hearts, with the lasting charm of a gentle and quiet spirit that is so precious to God."

NOVEMBER 6, 1998

Not long after that, he added notes on his study of the transfiguration to his journal. Most third graders would consider this a heavy topic. Not our BJ!

Today, I read [about] when Jesus took his disciples up a mountain to teach and speak to them. When he did, Moses and Elijah came down from heaven and talked to Jesus and God said through a cloud, "This is my son whom I love and am well-pleased in, listen to him!" And after that, it was just the disciples and Jesus.

I think that the disciples were terrified when that happened. It seems really awesome to us, which it is, but if we put ourselves in the disciples' shoes, we would be terrified. I can't imagine God actually speaking to me, saying, "This is my Son, whom I love, listen to him!"

DECEMBER 9, 1998

A young BJ

BJ's knowledge of Scripture impressed those who knew him even casually. It awed and inspired those who knew him well. One of those was his grandmother Higgins, who knew him better than almost anyone else in our family.

After Grandpa passed away, BJ claimed special time with Gramma whenever she visited. When my father died, a new era began in BJ's life.

He developed a very close relationship with his gramma (my mother). I believe my mother is one of the few people who understood BJ's depth. You see, after my dad's going home to be with Jesus, a new tradition started with BJ and Gramma. When she came to visit, Gramma would sleep in BJ's bed and Beej would sleep on the floor in his room. They would talk far into the wee hours of the night. My mom mostly listened, but she heard and saw deep into BJ's heart. . . . Before his bedtime, he would whisper to her, "Don't be too long; I wanna have time to talk."

He shared so many things with her. Some hurts, some joys, and some mundane things. These were precious times to them both. Both grew from this experience. Gramma kept most of his secrets, but occasionally would clue us in to things we "needed to know."

Dad, blog posting
October 7, 2005

I wish I could have recorded some of his conversations! I was deeply impressed at how mature his thoughts were. He would talk about having layers to his thoughts. In his prayers and comments, he would have such a deep spiritual aspect for a little boy.

I was just so interested! I taught elementary school and raised four little ones of my own, so I was just really amazed at times at the things he would say and his perception.

GRAMMA ETHEL HIGGINS

Others who knew BJ agreed that he knew and loved the Word of God. He showed this love by his constant study and the many questions he asked.

One of the things I so loved about BJ—and not because he's a relative, it was just the way he was—his faith was a very real faith. He was always asking all these great questions about the Bible, and I loved that. I never felt like any of that stuff was made up or said so that we would feel that he was spiritual: "Look at me; I'm being a good Christian boy."

BJ was very genuine, very God seeking. That's what I loved so much about him—the reality of his faith. He would ask things I never expected a young boy to ask, deep questions about God.

UNCLE RICH DANZEISEN

39

While still in elementary school, BJ began a journal that contains lists of Bible verses he used in witnessing and other lists from his own study, called "The End Times Scriptures, TEST." The inside cover of his favorite Bible, a New Living Translation, also shows his devotion to God's Word. Under "Favorite Verses," he listed: Proverbs 27; 1 Corinthians 15; "God is not a man (back)" (this referred to a dozen Scriptures written in the back of his Bible showing that God is not a man); "Predestination (back)" (again, referring to a set of Scriptures written in the back of his Bible); and finally Isaiah 6:8: "Here am I! Send me."

Even before reaching his teen years, BJ not only expressed his love for the Word of God but used it to encourage and teach others. BJ knew and relied on the Word for the wisdom that marked his life.

> He was the most spiritual, godly young man that I knew. Whenever he would start a conversation, he would always find a way to bring God into it. He would always be aware of what was going on.
>
> BJ was constantly encouraging me to go farther with God. He always had something to say if he thought maybe I was slipping. He would be there, and let me know that I was slipping. He would go into God's Word and bring me back up.
>
> TAYLOR DEBAUN, FAMILY FRIEND

> When BJ was about in sixth or seventh grade, he was always ahead of all the other kids. He could almost teach the Sunday school class, and sometimes his teachers even let him do that.
>
> BJ would always ask the questions that would intimidate the youth teachers. He was a challenge then, not because he was hard to teach, but because he wanted to know so much. Sometimes those kids can be a negative, a turnoff to the other kids—kind of a teacher's pet thing, but it wasn't that way with

BJ. All the kids respected him. They loved it when BJ taught. They looked up to him, even though he was the smallest kid in the class.

PASTOR RUSTY KENNEDY

BJ knew, loved, and believed God's Word wholeheartedly. As he grew older, he developed the ability to defend it—sometimes in an online forum.

By the way . . . While even I often have to stop and figure out something that the Bible says that may have previously been contrary to my beliefs, you're looking at the Bible the wrong way to say that when you find out about a portion of it, you disagree with it. Instead of only believing the Bible if it matches your own personal beliefs, make your beliefs match what BJ in 6th grade *the Bible says, because it has much more authority and relevance than our petty circumstances which bring about unsolid opinions. Many times my beliefs have changed due to finding a passage in the Bible that contradicted my old beliefs, but when this happens, do not assume that the Bible is wrong, assume that you are wrong. Because we are wrong a lot, but God is never wrong.*

HTTP://THENO1HANGOUT.PROBOARDS3.COM • MAY 28, 2004

Earlier, when challenged by someone who had compared the Bible to "a bigger fairy tale," BJ replied with his usual boldness.

Right . . . if it's fictional, then why does it perfectly match up with documented history? There is evidence that the man, Jesus from Nazareth, lived, taught, and was crucified. He is not some fairy-tale creature, nor was the entire history of the Israelites that is also documented in many other historical documents, which are again in perfect agreement with the Old Testament or Torah. You may choose to not live by the Bible or not believe it's true (pity you), but it wasn't written by Mother Goose, and certainly isn't fiction.

When pressed by someone else to be "a little more open-minded," BJ's response was equally blunt.

No, every thing that is in the Bible is fact, and I base my opinions on those. If u can show me something contrary to any of my beliefs from the Bible, I'll conform to it in a heartbeat. As for open-minded, truth isn't open-minded, it's a very narrow thing. And as for me possibly living a lie, I know I'm not bcuz I have found proof of God's existence that is sufficient for me, and besides there's this thing called faith . . . yeah that's believing sumthing that u can't see: thus God, and believing is knowing some particular thing is truth, not just saying "this is true for me, or I think it's true."

I will only condemn those that don't believe in Jesus Christ, and even then, I will still love them and try to be nice to them, bcuz it's God who ultimately condemns, not me. But I make it one of my goals (and this is based in Scripture as well) to tell them if they are living a lie.

But enough arguing about whether or not God is real or the Bible is truth, if u don't believe it, I can't really do much. Once the absolute truths are taken out of the equation, only God can stop u bfore u hit hell . . . to put it bluntly.

Like Jesus, BJ was able to use the Word to defend his faith. He could do this because, like Jesus, he knew the Word. How did he know it so well? He spent time in it daily.

> He was a very normal young man in most senses of what that means. He tried to develop a routine for when he would get into the Word, but it always seemed to fluctuate. At times, he would do it at school first thing, as he would arrive early, sit down in the cafeteria, and study. At times, he would do it as soon as he got home from school. At times, he did it before bed. The bottom line was that it was a priority, and he would make time. . . . [He] would just remember things. This included the Word of God.
>
> Dad, blog posting
> October 11, 2005

Higgins family at DiscipleNow

five

Ice to Fire

I went to camp with really high expectations, which scared me because I was afraid that it might not be as great for me this year as it had been for others in past years. In a sense, I guess I was challenging God. As I learned, God is *always* up for the challenge. . . . On Monday, the second day of camp . . . I prayed that God would reveal his will to me through the silence. It was then that I felt God leading me into the ministry.

Heed God's call.

A call to ministry. BJ had long waited, watched, and wondered if God would place such a call on his life. What exactly did that mean?

Ultimately, a great deal. His passion for God continued to grow. As he moved into sixth grade, he also moved toward a time when God would take his commitment to a new level. As he later said, he was passing from spiritual *ice* to the fervency of *fire*. He became known for that fire everywhere he went. Like young Samuel in the Old Testament, BJ learned early on how important it was to listen for God's call, recognize it when it came, and follow—every moment, every day.

> *I had recently accepted Christ as my Lord and Savior and invited him into my heart. With my new commitment, I began to really seek God and what he wanted in my life. I had been waiting for this time for almost five years, so it was truly a special time for me.*
>
> FROM "BJ HIGGINS"

First, BJ sensed God speaking to him through a series of sermons, Bible verses, and testimonies. All of them dealt with *"living your life for Christ and being real about it: not just going to church and going through the steps and rituals of being a Christian."* Eventually, he made the connection.

> *I realized that God was spiritually hitting me over the head with a two-by-four. I needed to change my ways and stop shaping my life around me and my own desires; but instead, I should have my life revolve around him. In response to my conviction from God, I prayed with my dad that God would give me strength to change.*
>
> FROM "BJ HIGGINS"

God's next fire-building tool: transition. After two and a half years of serving as associate pastor and youth minister at Crosswinds Community Church in Carmel, Dad gathered the family together. God had spoken. Dad didn't know just why, but he knew it was time to go—to step down from formal ministry and return to Northside Baptist Church.

My parents pretty much always talked about our entire family being called to one thing or another. When we went to Carmel, God called our family to serve there. Eventually, I started to sense that I was being drawn back to Northside. Right after that, Dad called a family meeting to tell us he felt like we were being called back to Northside too.

————
LAUREN

The change in churches came at exactly the right time for BJ. He sensed God's voice through the Northside youth group's Wednesday night Bible studies:

Every week, I seemed to be struggling with something different as far as being Christ-like; something I couldn't put my finger on. When Wednesday night rolled around, the lesson was often on that particular thing.

————
FROM "BJ HIGGINS"

The flame grew. God began preparing BJ for what Northside calls Ultimate Youth Camp, a retreat held each year in the Lake of the Ozarks area of Missouri—the camp where he described himself as "challenging" God.

On Monday, the second day of camp, after I did my quiet time, I prayed that God would reveal his will to me through the silence. It was then that I felt God leading me into the ministry. I then prayed that God would affirm my inkling if that was his will. Later that week, a speaker was talking about how God wanted to tell or reveal something to all of us that week. Realizing again the possibility of a call to ministry, I prayed for affirmation again. Once more, I felt God's calling when a [camp] devotional talked about what's next in your life. It was as if it was written specifically for me.

When ministry was brought up once more that week, I knew that God had affirmed me already, so I prayed for strength, and told my friends and mentors about my newfound call to ministry. . . .

After we got back from camp [I told the congregation about my call]. Now, I continue to grow in Christ, and towards that future ministry position. Whether [it] will be in the mission field, as a youth minister, music minister, senior pastor, or something else, I know who I'll be working for, even if I do not know what job I'll have.

FROM "BJ HIGGINS"

BJ rode with me in my pickup from Mamaw's house to our house. He was probably about twelve, maybe eleven. I was just amazed at how precisely and in how much detail he talked about what God was wanting him to do in life. As a twelve-year-old, I wasn't even thinking of the kind of things he was talking about. It amazed me how he really thought God was calling him to be either a missionary or a pastor. It wasn't like he was talking about something that he wasn't sure about. He talked with such enthusiasm about it, even at twelve years old. He was completely confident that God was going to do something special through him in ministry.

UNCLE STEPHEN TUCKER

As BJ sensed, his call to the ministry served as a milestone. He would give his life to serve God in his vocation as well as in his daily walk. Meanwhile, Dad continued to pray about his own calling. Where would the Lord send him next? He returned to a leadership role in Northside's student ministry, working alongside the associate pastor and minister to students, Rusty Kennedy.

At Northside, students have opportunities to do missions. Teams go out every summer, either in the United States or

overseas, to share the gospel. In March 2004 David Post, director of multimedia for Awe Star Ministries, was scheduled to visit
Northside to teach an evangelistic drama called "Freedom."
(Awe Star Ministries equips young people for life by providing them
with opportunities to serve others internationally. The ministry
also interfaces with churches who, like Northside, sponsor their
own mission trips using Awe Star materials.) During a weekend
retreat, David would train that year's student ministry team,
including Whitney Higgins, for a summer trip to the Ukraine. At
fourteen, BJ was not old enough for Northside's international
trips. He would have to wait his turn—at least, that's what his
friends and family thought.

> Rusty had to be out of town, so he asked me to take charge of
> the weekend. Big John [Hilfiker] was running sound and was the
> backup disciplinarian. At that time, I had every intention of going
> on this Ukraine trip myself. Later God showed me I was making the
> decision entirely on my own and that I shouldn't go.
>
> Dad

With Dad helping run things and Mom assisting wherever she
could, BJ hung around all weekend. He stood off to one side,
listening to David's instruction and watching closely. Silently,
carefully, he began practicing every role.

> We were here at Northside doing a drama rehearsal for a mission
> trip that BJ was too young to go on. BJ was up there. He was
> watching; he was doing every move that he could learn; he was
> just soaking it up. David Post, who was teaching, was watching
> BJ.
>   My youngest daughter had gone on a mission trip when
> she was very young, and I saw what it did in her life. During
> the break, David and I started talking, and he said, "That kid's
> incredible." I told him, "You know, I think he's old enough to go
> with you." That's when David started talking to BJ. I knew Brent

was pretty nervous about the whole thing. To me, it was just so obvious: BJ needed to go.

BIG JOHN HILFIKER

Saturday morning, BJ finally got his chance. Whitney had to miss practice to take the Scholastic Aptitude Test. David allowed him to stand in and play her role as the Knightmare (Satan figure). He loved it. He especially loved the sword fight between Satan and Jesus. Even after his sister returned to the rehearsal, BJ continued alone, practicing both sides of that complicated battle again and again.

Had the Father already begun to extend his call? BJ was moving toward the flame. As he had written earlier, "God is always up for the challenge." David Post spent that night with us and, on the way home in our car, began talking to BJ about the possibility of joining his own summer Awe Star team. Like the Northside group, this team would travel overseas. The team David and a co-leader were coordinating would also present the "Freedom" drama. This team would serve not in the Ukraine but in the cities and villages of Peru.

I told him, "You know, you're old enough to go with us." He seemed to think that would be kind of cool, but I didn't notice much reaction. He told me about a youth camp that Northside had. If he went on the mission trip,

BJ as the Knightmare
in 2004

he'd miss the camp and blow his chances for getting a perfect attendance medal they awarded.

DAVID POST, AWE STAR MINISTRIES COUNTRY COORDINATOR
PERU 2004, 2005

The biggest youth event at the church was Ultimate Youth Camp, and BJ had participated in that. . . . The remarkable thing to me is that, his first mission trip that he took—he knew [that if he went to Peru] he wouldn't be able to do youth camp or get that perfect attendance award later on. He sacrificed that—a tremendously spiritual time, a time of refreshment, a time of getting away, just being able to be ministered to directly with God. For BJ to have sacrificed that, to put himself in a place to be more ministering to others—that was a pretty big statement to me about his maturity. . . . It said volumes about his willingness to listen to God's direction and willingness to give of himself.

GLEN CHRISTIE

As David talked, BJ appeared laid-back, but he took the day's events and David's comments very seriously. That night he posted on his Xanga weblog:

My dad and sister had a drama training lock-in where I learned almost all of Whitney's and her arch-nemesis' parts. . . . OH! And I've been invited on a five-week mission trip to Peru this summer! For real! David, the dude who was teaching the drama ("Freedom") invited me. I'd be going with so far only seventeen other students from across the nation, ages thirteen to twenty-one, and would also be performing "Freedom" (in Spanish) for the Peruvians. It'd also be cool because the first four days of the five weeks is Spiritual/Mission/ Teambuilding/Drama training in St. Louis. The only problems? It costs about $2,800 and I would miss Ultimate Youth Camp. Tough decision, let's just see where God takes me . . .

MARCH 27, 2004

At lunch the next day, David told the other Northside students that BJ might join his Peru team. Their response amazed him. Immediately they began suggesting ways they could help BJ raise the money to go.

Big John, David, and BJ himself were now convinced that God had clearly called him. Big John assured Dad, "You need to let him go." At the same time, BJ came home, not asking but *telling* us, "Mom and Dad, God's called me to Peru, and I'm going!" By this time, any traces of ice had melted. The fire of his call burned pure and bright, and he was ready to follow in obedience.

We did not instantly agree with our enthusiastic son. However, we *did* agree to pray about the trip. These prayers brought God's quick response. He definitely wanted BJ to serve in Peru. But what about the cost? How could an unemployed eighth grader raise almost three thousand dollars? Awe Star's early payment deadlines, designed to help students raise funds gradually, had already passed. How could BJ possibly catch up?

Awe Star Ministries teaches students, "Where God guides, he provides." Once BJ confirmed his calling from the Lord, he moved rapidly to obey. He immediately filled out an Awe Star application and submitted it.

The next day a slightly frantic BJ called David Post. We were upset. He had mailed the application and the forty-nine-dollar fee in an envelope addressed to Awe Star—with no stamp. What should we do about the check?

A holy calm accompanies years of leading students overseas. David told him simply, "Let's just wait and see what happens." A day or two later, Cathy Moore (Awe Star's chief financial officer) brought BJ's envelope in with the mail. It had made the trip from Indianapolis to Tulsa—no stamp required, all contents intact. Once again, God was up for the challenge.

We have plenty of applications that take forever to get here or never come at all. BJ's was postmarked, but it had no stamp on it. We knew God had something special planned.

CATHY MOORE

BJ was up for the challenge too. He wrote a letter to potential sponsors and, for about two weeks, spent his evenings calling family and friends. He needed financial and prayer support. He asked for both. His Xanga site reveals his excitement:

God (may he be praised) is working in me more than he has in too long. I am entering a new spiritual "chapter" of growth and outreaching, leading up to my Peru trip.

MARCH 30, 2004

With his calling settled, the new chapter in his life unfolded quickly. By mid-April, BJ posted online:

So now I have all my Peru stuff done that I can do. I've sent out my sponsor letter thingies and both my applications, I've turned in my passport application, and am only awaiting a mission kit that I will get in the mail from Awe Star and $$ from sponsors. I also got an e-mail from one of the directors of Awe Star that included a list of people going. There will be seventeen people, including the director that leads it, any other leaders and myself. Also, out *of those seventeen, four (again, including me) are guys, and one (at least) is a leader.*

He wasted no time in introducing himself to his new teammates through a group email:

Hey, this is Brent Higgins (or BJ). I'm fourteen and this is my first mission trip, as well as my first trip out of the country. I live in Carmel, Indiana, where I lead a Bible study at my school, as well as one at my church (Northside Baptist). I'm sooo excited about being able to leave the comfort of my home and reach people for Christ in a foreign country.

I was saved on February 21, 1998, and I first realized that I am called into ministry in June 2002. My testimony isn't by any stretch a "drugs to glory" story. I (by God's awesome grace and blessings) grew up in a Christian home, and have always been involved with my church. However, despite much head knowledge that I had attained in my early years, I never really understood what Christianity is about until I was eight.

There's not much to say about my personality except that I tend to be outspoken about my beliefs (which, of course, are solely fixed on the Word), although I try to avoid useless debates, especially when fundamental beliefs are shared. I love swimming, climbing, going to church, and hanging out w/ God and my friends. I'm looking forward to meeting all of you. In Christ's Love, Brent

One by one, donations arrived. As BJ finished out the school year, he fanned the flame of his calling. More transitions lay ahead. Again, God was up for the challenge. Was BJ?

*N*ot called!" did you say? "Not heard the call," I think you should say. Put your ear down to the Bible, and hear him bid you go and pull sinners out of the fire of sin. Put your ear down to the burdened, agonized heart of humanity, and listen to its pitiful wail for help. Go stand by the gates of hell, and hear the damned entreat you to go to their father's house and bid their brothers and sisters, and servants and masters not to come there. And then look Christ in the face, whose mercy you have professed to obey, and tell him whether you will join heart and soul and body and circumstances in the march to publish his mercy to the world.

WILLIAM BOOTH, QUOTED BY BJ ON HIS XANGA WEBLOG
JULY 27, 2005

Section Two

The Passage

Peru 2004

Whoever wants to become great
among you must be your servant.

MARK 10:43 (NIV)

six

Rite of Passage

BJ Becomes a Man

For too long I haven't really been able to take myself seriously, and only saw myself as a boy, and *was* just a boy. Through being in the drama, feeling still like the little kid standing in for someone, and through just seeing my actions, I realized I was just a boy, and couldn't see myself or believe myself to be on a mission trip, much less lead as I know God has called me to. So, during worship, I prayed that God would transform me and raise me up to lead as a man.

BJ HIGGINS

PERU JOURNAL • JULY 19, 2004

Grow up!

BJ's training with Awe Star began on June 18. Neither he nor anyone in our family had any idea just how much those few days would change his life. God had already been at work to prepare him. BJ was ready to take a dramatic step toward growing up. The time was now.

Awe Star Ministries calls its training Awe Star University (ASU). In 2004 ASU took place at Hannibal-LaGrange College in Missouri.

We had some travel decisions to make. We could either arrange for BJ to fly to St. Louis or drive him to the training site ourselves. A family move made the decision more complex. In May, Dad had accepted a position as operations manager at Highland Lakes Baptist Camp in Martinsville, about forty-five minutes from our Carmel home. After we sold our property, we would live in a camp-owned house.

Even without an extra trip, this was obviously a crazy-busy time. However, a small group from Northside Baptist happened to be heading to the Lake of the Ozarks area, preparing for the annual Ultimate Youth Camp. As part of the youth leadership, Mom and Whitney were traveling with this group. They would drive through St. Louis on the exact date that Awe Star training began!

Arrangements were made for BJ to travel with the Northside team. They would drop him at the St. Louis airport, and the Awe Star staff would take him on to ASU. God had arranged his travel plans. As BJ himself would have put it, "Awesome."

BJ was just so excited that morning. We could all see it. We had spent the night with Brent at our camp house, and we had about a six-mile drive from there to the I-70 truck stop where we would connect with the Northside convoy. We knew BJ was called and ready, but he suddenly seemed awfully young.

On the other hand, he didn't seem concerned about leaving us at all. He had already been online talking to some of his Awe Star teammates, and he couldn't wait to get there and make connections.

Mom

BJ impressed me because he wasn't nervous at all. I remember feeling really bad for him because he was going to have to sit in the airport for a couple of hours with a person he didn't even know! When we got to the St. Louis airport, we all walked in with him. I remember thinking how crazy it was: the only information BJ had was to find a guy wearing some kind of red shirt with a cow on it (Awe Star's theme that year was "Sharing Jesus till the cows come home").

None of that seemed to bother BJ. He was ready to go. We hugged him, and I think we were nervous and excited for him all at once.

————

WHITNEY

BJ spent a couple of hours at the airport with Cody Smith, an Awe Star alumnus and summer staffer. After other student missionaries arrived, they all made the drive to Hannibal-LaGrange.

ASU goes well beyond traditional missionary training-in-a-box. Students receive information about cross-cultural ministry. They eat. They worship. They share devotional times with leadership. They talk about their faith. They pray. They spend countless hours practicing the "Freedom" drama. They fall into bed exhausted. First and last, they hear strong biblical teaching.

Through the years, Awe Star's president and founder, Dr. Walker Moore, has refined this training. His intentional design is that ASU prepare student missionaries not only for their coming trips but for lifelong service to the King. The impact of this intense discipleship on BJ's life was nothing less than profound.

June 18, 2004; Hannibal, Missouri
People I met today: Cody, Hannah, Chris, Pete (prayed with, promised to pray for me for focus), David, David, WALKER, Philip, my Peru team

How God worked in my life today: *God blessed me today through, first of all, the energy and adrenaline I needed to run all day on three hours of sleep. Second, through giving me TONS of time just to spend worshiping and praying to him, and his Word. Third, God blessed me with allowing me to meet and get to know several awesome Christians. When I first arrived, nervous, I met Cody, who was very friendly and (without knowing it, perhaps) eased my nerves somewhat. Fourth, through the way people have embraced and affirmed me. Fifth, he blessed me through worship and through the message, just completely speaking to me and giving me strength.*

Another Awe Star distinctive is that, though the ministry provides missions opportunities for young people, it is *not* a teen mission organization. Early in ASU, Walker Moore tells the students that he cannot take teenagers overseas. He asks them to picture groups of teenagers, dressed in Christian T-shirts and blue jeans, running up and down the halls of a youth hostel in another country. They spray water everywhere and wreak havoc before heading out to share the love of Jesus.

As a longtime youth pastor, Walker knows that picture very well. He has dedicated his life and ministry to creating a new one. Immediately BJ embraced this teaching. Once again, God had prepared the way.

BJ had always been the youngest child, the little brother. Now he was asked to be a man and do a man's work. It was not a coincidence that, several months earlier, a mentor had sent him home with Robert Lewis's *Raising a Modern-Day Knight* (Focus on the Family, 1997). Both he and Dad read the book. Like Walker's teachings, it explained the importance of taking a definite step from childhood to adulthood—a rite of passage.

During ASU, when Walker invited students to become adults, BJ was the first to move. At fourteen years old, five feet two inches, and barely over a hundred pounds, he was ready to grow up. He was ready to become a man.

> *June 19, 2004; Hannibal, Missouri*
>
> *Walker's lesson was on becoming and acting adult. He said that God's will has no adolescence and that we can't afford to take an adolescent on the trip. Then he called for those who desired to leave adolescence, experience a rite of passage, and become an adult to stand, pray, and promise it to God. God anointed this, and now I know that I am a man of God—through God—and not a boy.*

Awe Star training also emphasizes another aspect of growing up: leadership. David Post stressed to the team that, in Peru's male-dominated culture, the men should take the lead in shielding the women from danger. This was another concept with which BJ, always very protective of his sisters, strongly identified. Even during the training time, he was beginning to walk out his calling day by day.

> *June 20, 2004; Hannibal*
>
> *Kings 19:19–21; 1 Tim. 1:3–19*
>
> *Subject: Elijah, sin's mirror, Peter heals a crippled beggar*
>
> What God said to me: *Just as Elisha left everything to go with Elijah because he was instructed to, we need to be willing to leave everything for Jesus.*
>
> *In verse 6 [Acts 3], Peter said to the crippled beggar, "I don't have any money for you, but I'll give you what I have." This should be our attitude: a) an attitude of giving to one more needy, even if we have little, and b) an attitude willing to witness and help people at all times.*

As Christians, we should spend less time trying to live by the law or avoid doing wrong things, and spend our time instead trying just to be like Christ.

What I said to God: *God, please help me to focus solely on you and not on myself, Father. God, please help me to lead as a man; please work and live through me today and every day. Father, I surrender to your will, do what you want with me, and help me to be more willing to follow you.*

BJ was growing deeper in the Lord that whole trip. When we taught, he didn't want to play—he soaked everything in. You could see him soaking it all in, and he was stepping up to the challenges we gave. Our training enhanced what he already knew.

We always teach the students that it's important to walk out who they are in Christ. BJ wanted to be known as more than just a little kid.

———————
DAVID POST

June 21, 2004; Hannibal

How God worked in my life today: *Today, God taught me so much about being a man, about temptation (below and above voices) and my spiritual anatomy (body, soul, spirit). This morning all the men gathered to answer God's call to leadership. Then God taught me much on authority and the above-mentioned topics. . . . My prayer for tomorrow is that God would work through me and help me to lead even more as a man of God, and that I might be able to focus solely on him.*

God calls some amazing young men and women to serve with Awe Star Ministries. Many have taken hold of God's Word and the teachings gleaned throughout their mission experience. Their lives express incredible devotion. Ultimately, the world becomes their mission field.

Sam Beer is that kind of man. When he began serving with Awe Star, he was even younger (thirteen) and smaller than BJ. He says that because of his background, he watches for the younger guys at ASU. He knows their first international mission trip will be completely different from anything they've ever done before.

I heard people talking a lot about BJ, and when I spent time with him at training, I saw God's hand on him. I knew God wanted him to lead the team [serve as a spiritual leader for the group] even though he was the smallest and youngest.

The night before the teams left, I went to his room and said, "I have seen God at work in you. His plan for you is to be a leader—and lead by example—lead through servanthood and humility." BJ would be an example of a godly man. Before I left his room, I prayed with him. I knew he was ready for leadership [by example] on the mission field.

BJ and some of the Peru 2004 Team

SAM BEER • PERU EXTREME TEAM, 2004

June 21, 2004; Hannibal

How God worked in my life today: Man, today was awesome. After working on the drama all day, we had worship, in which we prayed with a small group of people sitting near us and learned about our identity, power, and authority in Christ. Afterward, each of the five teams took a turn being prayed for with everyone surrounding them in the middle of the room. We had to say goodbye to the [North Africa] team as well, which was a little sad.

*While I was in my room packing, Sam came and encouraged
me, saying he could see that God has his anointing on me, and
that he could tell God would do great things through me, and
then prayed over me. Then, when David was also in my room,
Pete came in and did the same. Several other people have also
encouraged me this way this week.*

A week or so after BJ completed his training, we received a
rare email from our son. He used his Internet café time to describe something very significant in his life: the rite of passage
process. We could sense his excitement as we read.

*From: Brent Higgins, Jr.
Sent: Wednesday, June 30, 2004 10:05 AM
Subject: To my family*

*Hey guys!! I'm in Piura right now; we arrived last night. I'm
having an awesome time here, I love all my team members and
everyone else that was at training—there are so many awesome
people, I can't wait to tell you about them all! Also, the Peruvians
break my heart how kind they are and how lost they are—their
god is just a piece of wood inside some building that they bow down
to every Sunday. I'm learning so much about leading, fighting
Satan's attacks (which are VERY numerous as we are doing God's
ministry), my walk with Christ, and memorizing Scripture, I could
go on and on.*

*When I come back, I will not be the little boy that you dropped
off all by himself at the airport. Two nights before we left for
Peru there was a sermon entitled "Missions: Danger. For Adults
Only." It was explained that this new Western culture of how we're
children, then adolescents from 9-26, then adults is completely
wrong, unbiblical, and not God's will.*

*Walker used several Scriptures to explain that . . . you go from
child to adult through one thing—a rite of passage. Then he went*

on to explain that we couldn't afford adolescents on the mission field. We needed to step up and embrace our significant tasks and become adults. At the end of the sermon he said, "Those of you who feel it's time to step up and embrace your significant tasks; become adults; and start to live, lead, serve, and act like adults, stand up so that I can pray with you."

Having just earlier that evening . . . prayed that God would change me from boy to man, because I knew I could not lead in my team, I could not minister in Peru as this boy that I knew I had always only been. I was the first to stand up, and then several around me stood as well. . . . So, long story short, when I come back, you will not find the boy you knew, but a man in his place.

seven

Armed and Dangerous

My leader from Peru did a lesson on this one of our first nights there, and it totally blew me away. It came from a passage I was familiar with—Ephesians 6:10–18. I knew about the different pieces of armor: Belt of Truth, Sword of the Spirit, Shield of Faith, Breastplate of Righteousness, Helmet of Salvation, Shoes of the Preparation of the Gospel of Peace. . . . I later began to understand even more of how essential, pertinent, applicable, and important that they really are to our lives.

BJ HIGGINS
FROM AN EMAIL • DECEMBER 31, 2004

Suit up!

BJ approached his life with enthusiasm. We like to tell stories of his early love for swimming. Our son thrilled at hurling his small body into the water to retrieve his favorite diving sticks—over

and over again. According to his autobiography, he played soccer with equal zeal.

> *I played soccer in the Northeast Youth Soccer League for many
> years. This was one of my most enjoyable activities. . . . I played
> as the main goalie on one team. At this time, I was even called
> "the animal goalie," because I would do anything in my power,
> following the rules, that I could to stop the opposing team from
> scoring. Often times, this would include jumping in front of a ball,
> and into the mud, while it was raining.*

From "BJ Higgins"

Anyone who knew BJ knew that when he embraced some-
thing, he gave it his all. He was never just *interested* in something
or someone. Instead, he was *passionate*.

This showed in BJ's love of swordplay. For most of his life,
he and his uncle Rich Danzeisen engaged in fast, furious, and
fake battles almost any time they got together. Their favorite
jousting method was Star Wars style, using toy light sabers.
Rich's son Joshua (nine years younger than BJ) later picked up
this tradition.

> Joshua always felt as though he was the same age as BJ. BJ
> was so good to play with him. He did anything Joshua wanted
> to do.

Aunt Lynae (Higgins) Danzeisen

Cousin Joshua and BJ

That's what I loved. When we would play light sabers, he was always really careful with Joshua. When I would play with him, it would be all-out warfare. My knuckles would be about three times their normal size because I would get busted up, and he would get busted up. That's the part I'll miss forever, having a friend who was always encouraging me to pursue the Lord, and at the same time determined to bust my knuckles with his light saber!

Uncle Rich

It seemed only right that BJ make the leap from mock battles to the kind that, although invisible, were much more real. Once again, God began with BJ's heart. Even before he realized it himself, others could see it. God was up to something big.

Brent [BJ], I am so proud of you—you are such a Christian soldier! Always remember to keep your faith in Christ strong and your motives pure. Keep sharing with others so that Christ Jesus is glorified!

Uncle Brad Higgins

DEDICATION IN BJ's JOURNAL, GIVEN ON HIS NINTH BIRTHDAY

He was really very well-rounded. He had such a unique and special relationship with God. He was very much a normal teenage kid, but with an incredible calling on his life. He knew that he knew God, and that God spoke to him.

Aunt Lynae

Although ASU ends when students leave for the mission field, discipleship training does not. Spiritual growth kicks into high gear as the Spirit of God applies God's Word during the teams' international journeys. BJ's experience was certainly no exception.

Even before BJ's time with Awe Star, Satan surely considered BJ a threat. His passion and commitment to Christ made him a bold and dangerous warrior. Now, however, he began to learn more specifically about the protection he would need to serve the King even more effectively.

Later, he wrote briefly in his personal journal about the importance of this battle armor:

SUIT UP! Ephesians 6:10–18
First: Fasten tightly the belt of truth to hold you up.
—Turn to God's Word and servants to find the truth on uncertain matters.
Second: Put on (and repair) the breastplate of righteousness to guard your heart.
—Focus on God; strive to live like him. Realize and remember that you are righteous and strive to live it out.
Third: Prepare for battle by putting on the Gospel of peace as shoes.
—Daily read God's Word and understand the Gospel so you are prepared if you fall. Begin memorizing Scripture again.
Fourth: Take up the shield of faith to quench the fiery arrows.
—Trust God in all you do. Believe that he protects you and will guide you. He has everything under control, so be courageous. "He is who he says he is, and will do what he says he is going to do." Then Satan cannot pierce you with doubt and worry.
Fifth: Secure the helmet of salvation to protect your head.
—Turn back to God. Realize and remember that he has forgiven you. Remember who you are. Remember your calling.
Last: Take up the sword of the Spirit—the Word of God.
—Use Scriptures, God's Word, to actively attack sin and defeat Satan's strongholds. Fight! This is war!

Awe Star requires students to spend daily time in God's Word. During training, they learn to use a quiet time journal to record the insights God gives. They also keep a global passage journal to keep account of the ways God works through them. BJ's journaling habit was well established before he went to Peru. This helped make his journals especially complete.

The 2004 Peru team began its ministry in Tumbes, a dusty coastal city near the Ecuadorian border.

> *June 23, 2004; Tumbes, Peru*
> *Phil. 4:8–13*
> *Subject: Joyful living*
>
> *What God said to me: Before I even read the devotional, God is speaking: We do not need to concern ourselves with these petty worldly comforts, for through and in Christ, all things are possible and probable. Christ is everything and we need nothing else. He is our comfort, our necessity; he is that "much" that sustains us while we have "little." We do not need to worry ourselves with these little problems and circumstances, for it is all in Christ's hands. We need to have the attitude of Christ and of Paul. Everything is loss anyway next to Christ. I count everything loss next to and for Christ. To live is Christ, and to die is gain. Hallelujah.*

> *June 24, 2004; Tumbes*
> *Matt. 5:27–30; Acts 3:12–26; Acts 4:1–22*
>
> *What God said to me: To spiritually "get rid of" sin, we must see it as useless, threatening our life, and already dead. And with the help of Jesus, we can get rid of it. . . .*
>
> *What I said to God: Father, take these sins from me, God, and give me your eyes. . . . Father, please give me focus, that I wouldn't be distracted, and keep*

BJ during his quiet time at Ultimate Youth Camp

our team and minds unified, and protect us from the certain attacks of the devil. . . .

How God worked in my life today: *This morning Sam came into David's and my room and encouraged us, taught us, and prayed over us. Then, as we practiced the drama in the Plaza de Armas, and the Peru Extreme team shared Christ with the people, several people came to Christ. . . . Then for sightseeing we took some boats out into the Pacific to an island and were walking around it, and Michelle (El Diablo) got stung by a stingray and was taken to the hospital, afterwards finding out she couldn't be on her foot for three days, so I have to take over her role for five days.*

Michelle's injury came as a surprise—but not to God. Another Awe Star saying, taken from the teachings of Walker Moore, is "Our disappointment is his divine appointment." When things don't go as anticipated (and they hardly ever do), student missionaries know that they must watch carefully to see what God has planned instead. The teaching and experience they receive on the mission field teaches them firsthand how to suit up in their spiritual armor as they prepare to withstand Satan's vigorous attacks. They also learn to watch as God brings himself glory, even through things like a painful stingray wound.

In this case, although God did not cause the wound, he knew all along that the team would face this moment. He had specifically prepared BJ to assume Michelle's part as the Knightmare in the drama. After all, why else would a student who was too young for the church mission trip spend so much time memorizing his sister's role?

God continued preparing BJ for battle. He would need every piece of his armor to meet the challenges of the days ahead. Although he had learned the part back in March, the Knightmare role is one of the two most complicated parts in the "Freedom" drama, and BJ had not yet practiced this role with the Peru team. He had some catching up to do—and fast.

June 25, 2004; Tumbes

John 15:8–17; Psalm 117–118:9 (Psalm—believers pray for courage, a sign of the coming judgment); Ezekiel 5; Acts 4:23–31

What God said to me: *I need to not just seek the harvest, but continue sowing and planting and watering seeds, for when Christ said "the harvest is plentiful, but the workers are few" he did not mean just harvesters or reapers. Workers include sowing, planting, and watering as well. . . .*

How God worked in my life today: *Inviting people was great. We learned some Spanish and the people were friendly; it was a great time. Then, it was fun, but sweaty, busy and hectic time, but I did successfully learn it [Michelle's role] in under 1 1/2 hours! The drama at San Jacinto wasn't very well done . . . but the response was a disaster—kids flooding us, crowding around us, and tugging on us EVERYwhere, and not one decision or evidence of planted seeds, although perhaps a few seeds were sown that we don't know about yet.*

Then, after we arrived back at the Plaza in Tumbes, we found that rather than opening for a festival that was going on, we were closing. So we sat and waited for two hours, not knowing when we would actually go. Then, we performed the drama in front of about 1,000 people, and MANY came to Christ, and countless more seeds were planted.

BJ and the team had just experienced God as Lord of the harvest. He always allows reaping at exactly the right time.

Their ministry in Tumbes continued. So did the challenges. Whenever God wanted to use them mightily, new obstacles arose. BJ and his teammates were still learning about the importance of suiting up—day after day after day.

Dear Higgins family, I was with BJ last summer on his first mission trip to Peru. He truly amazed me because though he

was so young, he . . . was such a strong man of God. . . . Not only is he a great friend, always encouraging me never to let my armor down, but also a dear brother in the Lord.

HANNAH DEGUZMAN, STUDENT MISSIONARY
PERU 2004 • BLOG POSTING • AUGUST 29, 2005

June 26, 2004; Tumbes

How God worked in my life today: This morning/afternoon, David taught, once again compellingly, on putting on the full armor of God. Then we went and invited people. . . . We met a group of men from the military, one of which when we/I shared Christ with, we could tell he wanted the relationship, but his friends thought it was cheesy, so he did not receive Christ. . . . God through me led a man (also from the military) to Christ, but just as God was working, Satan was too. As bats flew overhead and crowds of kids swarmed us, and the aforementioned English-speaking man talked to us for ten minutes, avoiding all spiritual or half-spiritual subjects. We struggled to overcome distractions (obviously from Satan) and present the gospel.

As the ministry in Tumbes moved forward, God built the team spiritually. Still, Satan did not lessen his attacks, confronting the young missionaries at every turn.

June 28, 2004; Tumbes

Psalm 118:10–18—This passage illustrates how through God, we can accomplish all things. It shows God's awesome power and strength and that he will protect us and destroy our enemies. Verse eighteen also sticks out because it illustrates that we have many trials and persecutions, are tested and even punished, but even so, it is only God making us stronger, and he is still on our side.

The same day that BJ wrote this journal entry, one of his teammates suffered a severe asthma attack. Leaders took her to the hospital. Within a few hours, another developed a high fever, and a third had already injured her ankle. BJ recognized the spiritual source of these physical struggles:

My prayer for tomorrow is: *God, just give our team focus, and give our men leadership in servanthood and humility. Father, let us live for you, in everything we do, just for you and you alone. God, remove Satan and his attacks from our team and from our presence. And in everything, may your name be glorified.*

When the team was in Piura, another northern city, God again used his Word to arm and encourage BJ.

BJ with Hannah, Matt, Courtney, David, and Ashley, Peru 2004

June 29, 2004
Isaiah 40:28–31

What God said to me: *I love this passage. . . . It paints a beautiful word picture: "They will mount up with wings as eagles, they will run and not grow weary, they will walk and not be faint" (Isaiah 40:31). Being a person who loves the majesty of eagles and flying, to say that if I trust in God, I will mount up with wings as eagles—man, that rocks my socks off. Also, the way it shows our weakness (v. 30) in comparison to God's strength. It also pertains to much of our troubles on the mission field right now. We are becoming tired, weak, injured, and sick, but GOD gives us strength, as it says here in Isaiah, we will soar with wings like eagles!*

The mission trip was only one-third complete. BJ and his Awe Star teammates had understood from the beginning that they fought against far stronger forces than stingray wounds, illness, or bats flying overhead. As their journey continued, so did the battle. As the battle continued, so did their focus on the One whose victory is certain—and eternal.

eight

Audience of One

I was going to type out all the things I have neglected to record in Xangaland lately, but then I heard my sister playing "Here I Am to Worship" and everything that once felt important to say fades. . . . God rocks, and he loves us, despite the fact that we continually spit in his face. We lose faith when faced with only slightly difficult circumstances, and turn from him on the drop of a hat, but he still loves us and will always be there for us. The LEAST we can do is just worship him.

BJ HIGGINS
WWW.XANGA.COM/DEADSILENCE7 • JUNE 2, 2004

> Worship God alone.

BJ and his teammates needed the protection of spiritual armor for the challenges they faced in Peru. They also needed something else. Like all those who seek to follow Christ wholeheartedly, they had to maintain their focus on an audience of One.

76

Awe Star prepares its student missionaries for reality. When they present the "Freedom" drama, sometimes the crowd will be sparse. At other times, hundreds will watch. Regardless, the team must learn to focus on God—the audience of One in and for whom they do all things.

BJ accepted this teaching as if it were his own. Even during his childhood, people noticed that he had a special sensitivity to God's Spirit and an amazing ability to praise him. He understood (far better than many adults) just how essential true worship is.

> I remember one time—our whole family had stopped at a camp with his family and one other family. We had worship times together. What I especially remember about BJ is that this was the first time I realized that he was just very honest in worship and everything that he did—honest and sincere with the Lord. I remember thinking that was pretty incredible. I saw this little kid who was more in touch [than the rest of us] with worshiping God. It was just an amazing thing.
>
> BIG JOHN HILFIKER

Also during his childhood, BJ began what became a regular practice—writing songs that expressed his deep love for God. He recorded lyrics for more than forty of them in his journal and elsewhere, sometimes even on scrap pieces of newspaper.

Worship music had long been a family distinctive. Mom, a music teacher, often used her gifts to minister at church. Lauren and Whitney, both self-taught on piano and guitar, also used their music in worship. Even Dad (who claims no musical talent) played the cello in junior high and sang on the praise team at Northside. BJ

BJ worshiping

loved to sing and, while he was in middle school, began learning to play the cello.

> We were so impressed with BJ's junior high orchestra. In the past, with kids of that age, you'd just hear them screeching around. I was just amazed at the quality of their sound. At age twelve, he played the cello for the seventieth birthday celebration the family had for my twin sister and me. BJ accompanied his mother and sisters on cello as they sang a song that Brent [Sr., Dad] had written.
>
> GRAMMA ETHEL HIGGINS

Like the rest of our family, BJ found ways to combine his love of music and worship. He used his knowledge of the cello to teach himself to play the bass and continued writing songs. Just one month before he left for Peru, he and some close friends had formed their own worship band. BJ named the group Ice to Fire.

> *Yes..... I'm finally in a band—for real! ... In it is Jack Meils on electric guitar; my brother, Taylor, on acoustic/electric guitar; and yours truly on bass! All we need is a drummer, and I have one on my mind that we're praying about.*
>
> WWW.XANGA.COM/DEADSILENCE7 • MAY 16, 2004

The friends BJ mentioned, with the addition of drummer Ryan Fitzpatrick, had joined the Northside youth group about the time we returned to the church. True brothers in Christ, they shared joys and struggles. In fact, just before forming the band, BJ and Jack Meils had begun an online student forum as a way to reach nonbelievers. They bravely tackled issues including sin, sexuality, theology—even favorite brands of cereal (BJ went with Peanut Butter Crunch).

When BJ referred to Taylor DeBaun as his "brother," he meant it. In the front of one of his Bibles, there was a place to list family names. BJ recorded the names of his parents and sisters—and Taylor.

The Ice to Fire gang shared common passions: music, God, and leading others to worship him alone.

> *e are Ice to Fire: "Like ice, our hearts, God break us; In your fire, Father, refine us" (our motto). We're a Gospel Rock Band, and all about G-O-D! . . . We're all about God and live for him, so we aren't open to doing things that go against him and his commands and desires for our lives.*
>
> *You really want to get to know the band? Get to know the Person behind it. We strive to make our lives about God and God alone, so to really get to know us, you gotta get to know him.*

WWW.ICETOFIRE.COM • EMAIL FROM JACK MEILS • JULY 5, 2006

BJ's Peru 2004 team members shared these same passions. As they traveled from Tumbes to Piura, BJ recognized the need to focus on their audience of One.

> *June 30, 2004; Piura*
> *Nahum 1*
>
> *hat God said to me: Be still and know that I am God. Be silent and see that I'm still here with you. David taught on letting go of sins and distractions we brought from home, but I had trouble. . . . I know that God will fight my sins with and for me, and so I let go, because I trust him to direct my life. He is God, and he is with me.*

David Post, the Awe Star country coordinator, knew that the students could not fully focus on God until they let go of sin and its distractions. Even their spiritual armor would prove ineffective without this step. BJ and his teammates began living out what they learned.

July 1, 2004; Piura

How God worked in my life today: *Today was awesome although up till about 2:30 I was in a more difficult and intense spiritual battle than I have ever been in my entire walk with Christ.*

Starting with last night—an awesome and convicting lesson on giving all *things to God. . . . The whole night I was overwhelmed (on top of exhausted) and confused as I started to lose [the] feeling of God's presence, and an intense battle began in my soul. As I tried to let go, Satan started attacking me. . . . Despite, during, and after my problem, God saved twenty-eight people through my ministry team [Awe Star's three-student teams sent out to share the gospel after the drama presentation] alone today. Now, what was left of the battle is all out gone; and I am hyped for more ministry, fellowship, worship, and discipleship.*

July 2, 2004

What God said to me: *It doesn't matter how much I serve, how much I forgive, teach, disciple, lead or do anything else if my attitude is negative. I need to not only serve, but serve humbly and cheerfully and willingly.*

What I said to God: *Father, I thank you so much for today, and for allowing me to come here to Peru to live solely for you. . . . Father, I pray that I would be able to just focus on you and learn from your Word and your people.*

BJ knew how to worship. He had been taught about the audience of One. He prayed fervently for focus. So it came as no surprise that as he and his team stepped farther out in ministry, Satan began throwing even more distractions their way.

July 2, 2004 (continued); Piura

H/ow) God worked in my life today: *The first drama site
(another school) was crazy. The kids were so loud we could
barely hear the music (full blast) and they were . . . on the stage
and crazy. Afterwards we . . . managed to distract enough kids so
that Suzanne and Junior (Mission Team Leader and translator)
could go witness to a group of teachers that accepted Christ. . . .
Fourth site, the Spirit was really moving. My group led four boys
(teens) to Christ, and other groups were at least as productive in
planting and harvesting.*

BJ wrote that his most challenging moment of the day happened at that fourth drama site. What did he find so difficult?
He wrote that his greatest struggle was "performing for an audience of One."

Through it all, BJ maintained his heart of worship. In this
time of relative weakness, worship brought the strength he and
his team desperately needed.

July 4, 2004; Piura

H/ow) God worked in my life today: *I went to a Peruvian
worship service today which was interesting. . . . For the first
drama and a half, I was dead tired and getting worse and had a
bad attitude, but then I was able to give it all to God, and he filled
me up. . . . As always, tons got saved, praise the Lord. . . . Tonight
has been another big battle inside. There are so many things God
is teaching, but so many things I'm holding onto that I need to let
go, and as always, my pride gets in the way of everything.*

Pride. It was something BJ had struggled with throughout his
Christian life. Now he was beginning to understand why—and
to learn how to combat it. The Enemy uses pride to pull our attention away from God and toward ourselves. Awe Star teaches

that God uses prayer to restore proper focus. BJ and his team witnessed this, even in the midst of more unexpected events.

The next day, the team saw only a small response at the first two drama sites. At the third, they confronted another trial. Michelle, pores open and tender from the stingray wound, came to a sudden realization. She had already become so sunburned that she was unable to wield her swords for the Knightmare role. There was no time to switch parts and costumes that quickly, so the team did not perform. Instead, a few students spoke to the crowd, and then all headed out for ministry.

July 5, 2004; Piura

How God worked in my life today: My group alone saw God save at least fifteen adults. Grown men were acting like children to get response cards and tracts. Phil and David O. were called across the street to the police station—security wanted to talk to them, and he (security dude) was led to Christ, then thanked and saluted them.

The team remained in Piura, traveling out of the city to minister at various sites. God continued working. So did Satan, using more illness and injury to attack BJ and his team. Awe Star was forced to cancel some planned dramas, but God continued to focus the team on their audience of One.

BJ and David as the Knightmare and Good Prince

Then on a free day, the team traveled back to Trujillo. BJ was sick and vomiting, but he was able to place his focus where he needed it most.

July 9, 2004; Trujillo

I was sick tonight. . . . I can't imagine what I would do if it happened at any other time than now, because for the first time in my life, I was able to focus on and turn to God as Scripture came to my mind and comforted me, like Revelation 21:4 and Philippians 1:21–24. Also, I most missed my dad tonight. . . . But then, a comforting thought came to my mind, and I almost cried: my Daddy was there with me and wanted to gather me up in his arms and hold me, that is, God. He got me through it.

A few days later, with Trujillo as home base, the team traveled to Pacasmayo, a coastal city two hours to the west. They also had several more days of ministry in Trujillo, sharing and seeing people come to the Lord without the active opposition they had experienced earlier.

The prayers BJ included in his journal during his final days of ministry there reflect his spiritual growth during the trip. He was winning the battle with pride by focusing his attention and allegiance where it belonged.

July 14, 2004; Trujillo

What I said to God: God, help me to focus on you and you alone. I have so much trouble getting distracted and absentmindedly letting my tongue loose. I pray that you would help me to keep a tight bind on it and stay focused and humble before you today. Father, please tear away any apathy that may linger along with any bad attitude or thing of me and not you. God, please help me to live for your glory, not my pride.

My prayer for tomorrow is: *God, please help me to be calm and focused and the man that you desire for me to be. Please speak through me, when I must speak and break me of any pride or things of me.*

July 17, 2004

*W*hat I said to God: *God, please give us focus today as we do our last day of drama ministry. Please help us/me to perform solely for you, and not be distracted . . . but just focus on you.*

July 21, 2004

*W*hat I said to God: *God, as I arrive for debriefing, please help me to not fall back to who I once was, God. As thoughts of self-glorifying come to my head, please destroy my pride once again. God, as the little boy tried to come back with his immaturity and sin, God, give me the strength to crucify my flesh each day and pick up my cross and live for you alone, as a man, a servant, a prince, following you. Help me not to rely on my own strength but on yours.*

At the beginning of the summer, BJ came in as a young guy that was eager to learn more about God. By the end of the summer, BJ was a man that was eager to help others learn more about God. He did not let anyone look down on him because he is young. He set a high standard for everyone. BJ's passion for God blew me away.

PHILIP TALLMAN, AWE STAR MINISTRIES TEAM DIRECTOR • PERU 2004

BJ had seen God do great things on this trip—in the lives of the people of Peru and in his own. He returned to the United States clearly centered on God. Just as in the "Freedom" drama, Satan had been defeated. Once again, BJ directed his heart and worship toward his audience of One.

Section Three

The Challenge

Therefore submit to God. Resist the devil and he will flee from you. Draw near to God and He will draw near to you.

JAMES 4:7–8

nine

Coming Home

Hebrews 12:1: "Therefore, since we are surrounded by such a huge crowd of witnesses to the life of faith, let us strip off every weight that slows us down, especially the sin that so easily hinders our progress." . . . Right now, I'm just having trouble stripping off *all* of the weights. . . . As embarrassed and annoyed and ashamed as I am that this is happening, I am slowing down, losing my passion for God, losing my thirst for the Word, losing my perseverance and determination to live for God, and losing my endurance and patience during trials. I am weak, giving in too easily to Satan's traps, and the worst part is, I know it!

BJ HIGGINS
FROM AN EMAIL • AUGUST 10, 2004

Turn away from sin.

As BJ and his team traveled to the United States together, their shared fellowship made a long flight much shorter. God had done it. He had used the weeks on the field to draw them closer to one another and, most important, to himself. Unfortunately, their Enemy was already on the prowl. As always, he would use every means at his disposal in an attempt to ensnare these returning missionaries in sin. Unfortunately, our son was not immune to his attacks.

Mission debriefing is a time for stories. Students who have served all over the world come back together, eager to tell what God has done. Awe Star teaches them how to do it well. Each student missionary writes a thirty-second testimony and several longer ones. As he prepared to come home, BJ's words reflected his own unique perspective.

30-second testimony:

Let me tell you what amazing things God has done this summer. Not only has God reaped an incredible harvest, he taught me who I am, and how to be who he wants me to be, and I would love to tell you more about what God did later.

3 minutes:

Peru is ripe for the harvest, and that's what God has been doing through us—reaping his harvest. We presented God's love to around a thousand people one time, and multitudes of seeking Peruvians came to Christ. Many times, ten or more adults came to Christ from just one ministry team. We were amidst the smell of trash and other similar smells of urban Peru; and there were multitudes of stray dogs and crazy drivers barking and honking repeatedly at us in the hot, desert-looking Peruvian cities; but all seemed to fall away when we were sharing God's love with people who wanted it so badly, they were often drawn to tears.

At one site in the city of Piura, we were unable to perform the drama, but we gave a few testimonies and sang anyway, then dispersed into the crowd that had gathered. God showed us at that site that he doesn't need us or our drama to do a mighty work. That day, I was able to lead about twenty adults to Christ, not to mention [the salvations God accomplished through] all the other ministry teams all around the plaza. This is just the tip of the iceberg of what God did in and through us.

PERU JOURNAL • JULY 21, 2004

During the one-day debriefing, staff and students share their stories. They also worship together, rejoicing in all that God has accomplished.

As the 2004 debriefing ended, we drove to pick up BJ at the host site, a St. Louis hotel. We were ready for him to come home. During mission trips, Awe Star permits students only two phone calls home: one when they arrive in country, the other at the midpoint of the journey. Filled with anticipation, we made the drive. Both of us were eager to see and hear from our son.

> I remember coming through the door into the hotel lobby and seeing a group of students standing there, talking and laughing. We kept going. Suddenly, we heard laughter behind us. We had passed right by without even recognizing BJ! That's why they were all laughing. They knew how much he had changed. They were all watching and waiting to see our reaction.
>
> Mom

> When he left for Peru, I think BJ had shaved maybe twice in his life. I'm not sure he even needed to do it then. When we looked at him that first day back, he seemed so different. God had brought an outward, physical manifestation of the inner spiritual change. He had long hair and a full beard. BJ looked like a man.
>
> Dad

We had read BJ's email about "coming home a man" with some skepticism. After all, this was our little (as Mom put it when BJ let her) "Beejie." Now he looked like a man, but how deep did the changes go? We would wait and see.

We didn't have to wait long. Throughout the next few days, BJ told story after story of God's work in Peru. Our only frustration was his stilted approach. His carefully memorized testimonies made him sound like a robot. Friends noticed this too. Everyone wanted to hear about Peru as BJ had experienced it—not through what sounded like a canned presentation.

> When he got back from Peru, there was a different sense about him. He almost had an arrogance about it. It was a holy excitement and confidence about seeing God do great things. It can come across the wrong way. Eventually, he got real with what God was doing. When he could get through the formal presentation side of it and it became real, he presented it in a totally different way.

> PASTOR RUSTY KENNEDY

As BJ's communication style improved, he had no trouble keeping his hearers' attention—as long as it wasn't too late at night. His passion was obvious. His inner battle, however, was not.

> *Since my last update, I went on a big family reunion, where I was able to share much of what God did on our trip. . . . So I just ask that you pray that God would empty me, that I may be a vessel of God, and that he would use me, and that God would give me strength as Satan attacks viciously with all kinds of apathy and distractions and temptations, and as I battle a new stronghold: impatience.*

> FROM AN EMAIL • AUGUST 5, 2004

I noticed a change in the way he spoke. He spoke with more passion and more fire in his eyes than I'd ever seen in anyone before. It was like something you could look at and you knew that he was unshaken. He was serious about his relationship with Christ, even more serious than he already was.

BRITTANY DISALVO, FAMILY FRIEND

When he got back from Peru that first year, there was so much more purpose in what he wanted to tell you. He liked to give you the long version of things. When he got back, it was much more than that. It was very important to him that you understand that he wasn't just telling a story to entertain you.

Not long after he got back, we had a family reunion in Wisconsin. We were sitting outside, and he started telling us about Peru. I finally went to bed about midnight. I don't know how many people stayed out there, but BJ talked for as long as anyone wanted to hear about that trip. He just truly had a passion for sharing.

That was the first time I ever saw that passion at that level. I knew his faith was important to him; I knew he had a very real relationship with the Lord and that he had a real concern about his friends. But now, it was just really up several notches—his level of intensity—in what he was saying and his desire for you to hear more than just the words he was telling you. He wanted you to be there with him—to see and hear and experience what was happening.

UNCLE BRAD

We told him that we were interested in hearing about his trip. . . . His excitement and passion were obvious. Deanna was exhausted after a drive from Wisconsin, and [BJ's uncle] Dan was beginning to get sleepy. After quite a while, BJ

Cousin David and BJ sharing a Mexican meal

paused, and Dan said, "Thank you for sharing, BJ." AND THEN, BJ said, "And then we traveled to this other city . . ." and his sharing continued! (We were in actuality about half through.) He didn't seem to notice the droopy eyelids of his audience. It was precious!

AUNT JOLENE TUCKER • BLOG POSTING • OCTOBER 4, 2005

God had worked mightily in BJ, but sin was crouching at the door. It made great inroads through his dissatisfaction with our recent move. Our house had sold while he was in Peru. When he returned, we drove him to our new home at Highland Lakes Baptist Camp in Martinsville.

Had he really come home? BJ felt incredibly torn. He knew that God had called his dad to the camp ministry. He had learned in Peru that God could use him powerfully, regardless of his location or circumstances. However, he was leaving close friends— even brothers—back at Northside Baptist Church. He had no established ministry in Monrovia. Then we broke the news that we could no longer transport him for the Ice to Fire practices. He would have to quit the band that he, Jack, and Taylor had started only weeks before his trip.

At first, BJ allowed the changes to overpower everything else. He moved almost instantly from stunning victory to crushing defeat.

I'm utterly broken and torn apart. God has called me to a new place, new people, new ministries, a new youth group with my move, but though I know God's will for me is here, I desperately want to be elsewhere. I want to go back "home" to Carmel, Indianapolis, my old church, my old friends, continue my ministries there. I feel like I just don't belong here.

FROM AN EMAIL • SEPTEMBER 15, 2004

> Once he started school, he became very defiant in his attitude toward us. He was frustrated with what he perceived as the poor academics there. He was upset when we made it clear that we couldn't drive him back and forth for band practice. After a few weeks, I had to sit him down for a talk. I told him, "As the spiritual leader of our family, God has called me to be here. You are going to be miserable until you decide to plug in here and see what God has for you."
>
> Dad

BJ was struggling. That much was evident. He had learned from Awe Star that true fellowship has nothing to do with food or buildings ("church fellowship," "fellowship hall"), and everything to do with sharing the things of God. On the mission field, the Peru team had learned the power of mutual confession and prayer. This Christ-focused fellowship had bound their hearts and lives together. Not surprisingly, when he sensed himself slipping, BJ again turned to his team to help him in his battle to turn away from sin. Now, he wondered: why had he waited so long?

Kay, I just want to ask for your prayers, because I just came/ am coming out of a HUGE spiritual battle. David meant it when he was talking about how this is a marathon and it only gets harder as it goes. It's amazing how easily Satan can twist little truths into lies and completely send you into a spiral of confusion, apathy, impatience, and all otherwise detractions from God.

The particular truths that he twisted in my case were with my parents and with my position. With my parents, he seemed to convince me that they didn't care about me very much; or if they did, didn't act like it. Also, with my position (regarding my location)—Satan tried hard to draw me away from Monrovia and back to Carmel and Indy. It got to the point that I was only a hair away from running away, which I've never had problems with. . . . It hurts me to look back and see the time I wasted, and the unnecessary efforts and failures when I had support one phone call away in multiple directions. But somehow, Satan convinced me that I didn't need to call. . . . I feel that the past week and a half or so, since I started school, have been sheer failures. Failure to let others know who I am, failure to fight off Satan's attacks. . . . However, I believe that the tides are about to turn.

From an email • September 3, 2004

BJ was right. In fact the tide was already turning. He was coming home. He would turn away from sin and move toward God once again. He had learned about this during his days of battle in Peru.

To spiritually "get rid of" sin, we must see it as useless, threatening our life, and already dead. And with the help of Jesus, we can get rid of it.

Peru Journal • June 24, 2004

The team prayed. God worked. By mid-October, BJ posted on his Xanga:

By the way, none of y'all in Indy will be seeing me in concert with Ice to Fire any more unless it's a guest-singing thing. . . . Another large aspect of happenings since my return is adapting to my new environment: Hicksville—ahem—Monrovia. For a long while, I wasn't doing very well. I refused to adapt; I left my heart back at Northside and Carmel, so to speak. Finally, I gave in and decided to actually seek God's will for me here rather than mope and complain about the move the whole time. My main problem was that I didn't feel that there was a place where I could plug in and use my spiritual gifts (knowledge, teaching, and service) or have an edifying fellowship. Of course, what I overlooked is that I

94

have to actually want these things, and seek God to find them. So I finally did, and guess what?—PRAISE GOD!!—He does have plans for me here.

www.xanga.com/DeadSilence7 • October 11, 2004

As BJ turned away from sin, God began to use him in ministry once again. His confidence and passion began to return. Later he reflected on what had happened, and he recognized more than ever the need to stay on guard.

Galatians 6:1 talks about what to do if someone is spiritually "overtaken" by sin. The Greek word used for overtaken there literally means, "to be caught off guard," and could also mean the person was at a vulnerable point. This is a clear description of what happened to me. I let my guard down at some point, and Satan attacked and attacked and attacked. Prayerfully, I learned my lesson, and am trying in every way possible to stay on guard, with ALL of my spiritual armor on (Ephesians 6:10–18).

But thankfully, I truly believe . . . that God is bringing me back; that God is waking me up again to the LIFE he has for me. So if you could, I would like to ask you to pray for me, as I know that the road ahead will be a rocky one, and that Satan is and will be attacking hard with all kinds of temptations. My prayer is that God will give me true strength, and that I will not fall again like I did before.

www.xanga.com/DeadSilence7 • May 12, 2005

BJ had come home. As God's plans unfolded, he would remember these lessons. He would strip off every weight. He would turn away from sin. He knew little of the race that lay ahead, but he would run with endurance. As he faced his next battle, he would stand up and fight—as a man.

ten

A Sword Unsheathed

I will not be satisfied.
I will not let my passion be held in a bottle.
I will not let my light be hidden.
I will stand up.
I will let my voice be heard.
I will lead, I will serve, I will fight.
I will tell people about Christ.
I will unsheathe my sword.
It's time to raise a revolution.
God will give me the strength.

BJ HIGGINS, 1989–2005
ADOPTED BY AWE STAR MINISTRIES AS ITS
GLOBAL PASSAGE CREED • 2005

Stand up and fight.

BJ made a fresh start. He had turned away from his attitude of discontentment. Once again, he began reaching out in ministry. Once again, he found himself engaged in battle. God had prepared him, both on the mission field and back home in Indiana, to stand up and fight.

We had always tried to stand alongside each of our children, supporting and strengthening their growth in the Lord. That fall, we did something special that meant more to BJ than we could have anticipated. It happened on his fifteenth birthday, October 1, 2004. His words reveal the dynamic impact:

As I was TRYING to sleep in, at 6:45 in the morning, my parents (the audacity!!) decided to WAKE ME UP singing happy birthday—However, they did not come into my room as I expected them to do, but they left my door closed, so I moaned, rolled over, and tried to sleep some more [while they left two boxes outside my door].

First, I will tell you of the smaller present—that is—the gigantic box. Definitely an awesome incredible stereo. . . . It's a five-CD disc changer, is just wicked awesome (if I may use that expression).

Second, I will tell you of the larger present—the smaller, long, cylindrical package on top of the stereo. . . . As I began to unwrap [it], I began to realize that it was, in fact, a sword. . . . It's single-edged except for the top three or four inches, and is about the sharpness of a steak knife. It also has a cool design down the blade, and some Middle-Eastern writing near the hilt.

Now, for the bigger, more serious side of the gift—as he gave it to me, my dad said, "This sword is symbolizing your coming into adulthood." It is this profound statement from my father that makes the sword, though smaller in size, bigger in value than even my wicked awesome stereo. It is not just that I really, really wanted a sword 'cause they're cool, but that my dad presented it to me, announcing his blessing on my coming into manhood. With the exception of the gifts that God himself directly gives, one could not ask for a greater gift.

WWW.XANGA.COM/DEADSILENCE7 • OCTOBER 11, 2004

When he did become a man, his parents bought him a sword—
that was to represent that he was all grown up now—that he
could handle himself. That sword was like the sword he could
always unsheathe and battle through the spiritual warfare or
whatever Satan threw at him.

Taylor DeBaun

Dear Brent Jr., Happy 15th birthday! You are a young man now
and proud of it, I'm sure. Congratulations.

I know this is an adjustment time in your life and not easy
for you. This lone seashell [on the card's face] reminds me of
how you might feel at times, but how it stands out! God cares
for it—and you in a special way. You have a chance to "shine"
in your environment, BJ. It can be a strengthening experience
this year. I hope and pray it will be and that many good things
happen.

Gramma Ethel Higgins

Hi baby brother. . . . I just want to let you know I think you're
such an awesome person. You have grown up so fast, it's cliché
but true. . . . I love you Brent. . . . I just wanted to let you know
that.

Whitney, message in BJ's personal journal

The gift of the sword, along with Dad's words and others'
affirmations, acknowledged God's work. The boy who left for
Peru had returned to face his future as a man. He would stand
up and fight for what he believed. BJ was once again opening
his heart, which had dulled in its sensitivity to the promptings
of God's Spirit.

However, he soon realized that he had another problem. Like
most of his generation, he loved video games. He began struggling with the amount of time he gave them, writing about it in
a school composition early in the fall of 2004:

I myself am a fan, as you could call it, of entertainment, which often means I am found passing time on an X-BOX or in front of a television set using excuses like "it's fun," or "it's interesting." Certainly there are exceptions . . . [but in general] the "entertainment industry" . . . centers around the wasting and making of time and money and is slowly robbing adults and children of productivity with an excess of "fun" and relaxation outside of required occupations and education.

Shortly after receiving his sword, BJ attended a youth retreat sponsored by Plainfield Baptist Church. The weekend emphasized the need for an awakening: a personal, radical awareness of God's transforming power. For BJ the timing was perfect.

Throughout the retreat, God spoke very clearly to him about his media attachments. In his "Awakening" journal, he listed "video games" and "media (TV, movies, news, Internet)" as things that numbed his mind and blocked his view of God. He also included "Girls" on this list. During middle school, he had struggled in an off-again, on-again relationship with a young woman. He knew God wanted him to make some changes—right away.

BJ used his retreat journal to record his heartfelt responses. He committed to fast from all forms of media for one month and to avoid any relationships with a "significant other" for one year. However, his final journal entry contains the most passionate statement of all (now adapted as Awe Star's Global Passage Creed—see the beginning of the chapter). Significantly, he signs it "James Timothy Christ." BJ had taken on this new name to show his complete identification with Christ and with other biblical

Resting before work in Corbin, Kentucky

role models (later, he used an even longer name, also ending in "Christ").

Self,

I will not be satisfied. I will not let my passion be held up in a bottle. I will not let my light be hidden under a bush. . . . I will stand up. I will let my voice be heard. I will lead. I will serve. I will fight. I will tell people about Christ. I will bring him up in conversations. I will not watch TV or play video games. I will not visit any but strictly Christian, beneficial Web sites and will only e-mail if it is edifying to a believer. I will fast from the telephone and the rest of media. I will memorize Scriptures again, read Christian books again, and spend more time in the Word. I will unsheathe my sword and stop playing all defense in this war. It's time to raise a revolution. I cannot and will not do anything mentioned above or anything otherwise. God will give me the strength and do these things through me. I will go forward at the invitation tomorrow.

    Brent Higgins, Jr./James Timothy Christ

October 23, 2004

The page of the retreat journal that carries these moving words also holds a printed quote adapted from the words of Martin Luther King Jr.: "You don't know what you're alive for, until you know what you would die for."

BJ loved to play video games. The time he spent on that or on the computer was a real sticking point. We argued about it sometimes—that if he were devoted to the Lord, he would spend less time on the games and more time with him. That fall BJ became convicted about this himself and decided to give it up. His relationship with God grew because it had become so much more important to him. He wasn't giving up something that was sinful—he was giving up something he enjoyed to spend even more time with the Lord.

—————
LAUREN

Almost as soon as BJ made these important decisions, he faced another dilemma. In an attempt to connect with nonbelievers, he had joined the school soccer team. It didn't take long for him to realize that the relationships weren't happening and the time commitment was too great. He quit the team. Soon, however, he began a sport he had never attempted: wrestling. Again, after a few weeks, he thought about quitting. This time, he persisted.

I think this says a lot about his character: he used to play soccer in high school. He quit because he just didn't have the time that he should have been able to put into it. He also wanted to quit wrestling, but he didn't want to seem like that kind of undependable person.

—————
JACK MEILS

BJ's own words about his wrestling experience were surprisingly brief:

I joined wrestling at my school, which I hated and dreaded for most of the season. But I finished anyway, and ironically won the "Mental Attitude Award," because I maintained a positive (or neutral) attitude at practice and meets.

WWW.XANGA.COM/DEADSILENCE7 • APRIL 5, 2005

As the winter wore on, BJ encountered another battle. The Enemy loves to take a godly desire and twist it. BJ longed to return to the mission field—but not to Peru. At first, he considered Awe Star's Uganda trip. He was too young. Almost immediately, he switched his interest to Thailand, where Awe Star was also sending a team. BJ saw this as a more difficult trip—right in line with his longing for risk. He had faced the challenges of Peru. Now, he believed, he was ready for something that would push him even farther.

God makes it clear that his ways are not our own. When our prayers about the Thailand trip did not bring peace, we felt uncomfortable about saying yes.

Our son, his heart already set, continued to struggle. His inner battle had outward effects that were obvious to us and to his sisters. BJ's personal journal again reflects this time of spiritual challenge.

> *Father* Father . . . *I feel I have fallen. I see my need to get back up, but I am reluctant. I don't want to get caught up in emotions or mimic a comeback for my glory or peace of mind. I sense strongly, however, that it is . . . time to come back to you. . . . Father God, prepare me for battle. Amen.*
>
> DECEMBER 30, 2004

Awe Star's David Post, so crucial in encouraging BJ to go to Peru, also had input in 2005.

> I called and talked to him a couple of times about going back to Peru. I did not know he was thinking about Thailand, but I called him and told him I needed a man on the Peru 2005 team who could be a leader.
>
> DAVID POST

Ultimately, BJ recognized the source of the problem. Characteristically, he analyzed it himself.

*D*iagnosis: "What did I do?"

• *Belt of Truth loosened, causing me to stumble.*
  —*Uncertainty on certain doctrines caused a little confusion.*

• *Did not prepare or shoe myself with the Gospel of Peace—put flip-flops on.*
  —*I slacked on staying in the Word and did not memorize Scripture.*

• *Without proper shoes, could not get up from stumble regarding the belt of truth.*
  —*I did not turn to the Scriptures to gain a firmer understanding of the truth.*

• *Disarmed, became more vulnerable to attack.*
  —*I was not paying attention to God, or Satan attacking me (dropped my guard).*

• *During fall, dropped shield of faith.*
  —*I stopped trusting God in everything.*

• *Breastplate of righteousness pierced, cracked.*
  —*My lifestyle altered, I became more irritable, depressed, cynical, less caring, more prideful.*

• *Helmet of salvation slipping.*
  —*My lifestyle corrupted, my desire for God gone, I stood on the brink of rejecting him altogether.*

• *Sword of Spirit in sheath.*
  —*I was not actively attacking Satan or my sin.*

PERSONAL JOURNAL • WINTER 2004–05

After BJ had suited up again in the armor he had learned to prize, he freely surrendered his personal desires. He made the choice to stand up and fight. He wasted no time in telling us of his decision.

What I remember most happened last spring when I came home from school. We were in front of the big window, and BJ was telling me about what God was doing in his life. He was telling me about how he was frustrated with his own falling away, and how he wished to be more sold out. He was finally getting back with God again. I was telling him the things God was doing in my life. I remember being really proud of him. My baby brother was challenging me spiritually.

LAUREN

Just as his struggles had been evident to our family, so were his joy and victory. BJ got it: a real warrior lives with sword unsheathed, ready to stand up and fight—to do his Master's bidding. BJ would follow him in obedience to Peru.

It was time to raise a revolution. God would give him the strength.

I was so amazed at the letter BJ sent out before he went to Peru the last time, telling what they wanted to accomplish. I couldn't believe he had written that letter. I asked Deanna, "Did BJ write that?" Of course she said, "Yes, Mother, he wrote that!" I always contributed and helped him any way I could. I was so proud of him.

MAMAW LOUISE TUCKER

Dear _____,

Last summer, I had the incredible opportunity to go on a five-week mission trip to Peru with Awe Star Ministries, and God did amazing things in the lives of the Peruvians and in the lives of my teammates. About one thousand Peruvians came to know Jesus as their personal Lord and Savior, and God totally transformed my life.

Well, this summer, God has called me back to Peru, and I can't wait to see what he is going to do. Once again, we will be *working in the northern areas of Peru, from the coastal desert to the Andes Mountains. The three cities that will be our "home base" are Trujillo, Piura, and Tumbes. We will also be performing the same drama, "Freedom," for the people. This drama outlines the Gospel and often gathers quite a crowd. . . .*

I would ask you to pray that God would prepare my team and me. We learned last year that team unity and spiritual maturity is crucial for the mission to have the greatest impact, but also that God's strength is in our weakness. In 2 Corinthians 12:9, God told Paul, "My grace is sufficient for you, for my strength is made perfect in weakness." So I ask you to pray that God would keep us humble, and help us to realize that it is by God's strength we can carry on and that an impact for Christ will be made.

LETTER TO FRIENDS AND FAMILY • APRIL 11, 2005

Section Four

The Return
Peru 2005

Let all that you do be done with love.

1 CORINTHIANS 16:14

eleven

Don't Waste Your Life

What is of great concern to me: the inauthenticity of people in general. . . . God is not religion, he is reality. God did not intend for us to be religious; he intended for us to follow him. . . . We should just try to get to know God, not just follow meaningless rules. We should also try to show others that God is far beyond these religious traditions and droning sermons. We should show them and be an example to them about how truly fulfilling, satisfying, amazing, and real God is when he is known and worshiped in true authenticity.

BJ HIGGINS
"WHAT IS OF GREAT CONCERN TO ME" • SCHOOL ASSIGNMENT • 2005

Make your life count.

After BJ had surrendered to God's call, the fund-raising for his second mission trip to Peru went smoothly. So did his remaining weeks of public high school. We had agreed to homeschool him beginning with his sophomore year, and he was excited. Although he would miss his friends at Monrovia High, he saw even more potential for ministry elsewhere. He had begun reading a book called *Don't Waste Your Life* in which author John Piper says: "God created us to live with a single passion: to joyfully display his supreme excellence in all the spheres of life. The wasted life is the life without this passion. God calls us to pray and think and dream and plan and work not to be made much of, but to make much of him in every part of our life" (John Piper, *Don't Waste Your Life* [Crossway, 2003], 37).

Piper's words captured BJ's priorities. He seemed to live each moment with a sense of urgency. Regardless of the situation, he never wanted to miss any aspect of God's purposes and plans. Making his life count for eternity was essential.

During the first part of June, before returning to Peru, he traveled with a group from First Baptist Mooresville on a mission trip to Corbin, Kentucky.

The group, which also included Mom, had two main ministries: restoring a mission house and holding a Bible club at an apartment complex. Although this seemed tame compared to what he would face in Peru, BJ put his all into the Corbin work.

BJ and Mom on Corbin, Kentucky, mission trip

he best part of the trip was getting to know the people in my youth group on a spiritual level and being able to just love and disciple the children that we spent time with. Since I [like to help out at the camp when I'm home], the service projects weren't out of the ordinary for me, though it's always awesome to see how God works through our service.

WWW.XANGA.COM/DEADSILENCE7 • JUNE 11, 2005

Every time we worked with the kids, BJ was with us. He had a lot of energy, a lot of enthusiasm. There was one little boy that they told us had trouble in school. BJ would always sit down with this little guy and take time with him. He also loved to teach the lessons—that was pretty much his thing in working with the children.

PASTOR LARRY FLOYD • FIRST BAPTIST CHURCH OF MOORESVILLE

On the mission trip one young man would be sitting by himself [on the church van], and the other seats would have three or four people crammed into them. One day BJ got in, looking for this same young man. He plopped down beside him and said something like, "How's your day going? How do you like the trip?" The boy answered, "Fine, except I don't have very many friends." BJ just stuck his hand out and said, "I'd like to be your friend," and kind of hung out with him the rest of the trip. He was an amazing young man, but also a very ordinary teenager.

CAROL JONES, FAMILY FRIEND

BJ was definitely ordinary. He teased his friends. He annoyed his sisters. He pestered his parents. When our family ate out, he had the habit of ordering the most expensive thing on the menu and never finishing it. BJ also talked—a lot. Often, when he was in the midst of a long discourse, Dad would interrupt in frustration, asking instead for the "short version." BJ always gave the same answer: "This *is* the short version!"

BJ was a talker. He could talk about anything!

MAMAW LOUISE TUCKER

I remember one time where I was having dinner with the family. They had to put BJ at a separate table, so he'd finish his meal and not talk!

WES CATE, FAMILY FRIEND

He was always so good at telling really long stories. It used to drive me crazy! People would always say how mature he was for his age. He sounded like he was twenty years old when he was only in about fifth grade.

WHITNEY

He was a typical kid but he had spiritual depth beyond his years and really had a heart for God and for others—but he was a typical fourteen- or fifteen-year-old kid. He forgot everything. No matter where he went, he left something there. We always talk about Deanna saying, "Well, son!" On the Corbin trip, the joke was that he had to have the last word on everything. It was like, "BJ, you can't say another word after we make this statement!"

CAROL JONES

People think BJ was a perfect kid, a perfect missionary—but he was still a kid. He was very spiritual, very connected with God, and he knew what he was doing. He was a normal kid, but he was very mature for his age.

BIG JOHN HILFIKER

Like his Awe Star teammates and family, the Corbin team saw two sides of BJ: a playful one and a spiritual one. Nearly every evening, the group went swimming in a nearby lake. BJ, who loved water sports, went along as often as he could. When it was

112

time to return to Indiana, he (like most of the other students) bought a Kentucky T-shirt. The one he chose was bright pink. He knew this would elicit a reaction from Dad, and he couldn't wait to see it.

> There was a large boulder-type rock right by the lake. It was probably twenty to thirty feet high. We had heard stories about kids who jumped off and broke a collarbone or a leg, so being a parent and a good pastor, I told them, "Nobody

Just being himself!

jumps off here. We're not gonna do that." BJ kept after me. He never won, but he kept after me. I remember him saying, "What's life without a little danger?" That was the essence of BJ.

PASTOR LARRY FLOYD

When the kids came out of the store, they had all these different shirts. Here comes BJ in a pink T-shirt, saying, "I can't wait to see the look on my dad's face!" When we got back to Indiana and got out of the van, BJ had on his pink T-shirt. There was Brent, shaking his head and rolling his eyes.

LOWELL JONES, FAMILY FRIEND

Just a few days after the Corbin trip, we told BJ good-bye once more. Intent on teasing his dad, BJ had left him a special Father's Day gift: a pink dress shirt. It awaited Dad's unwrapping—and amusement.

There is a time to laugh. There is also a time to work. A passionately focused young man headed to Dallas for his Awe Star training.

June 19, 2005; Dallas, Texas

What I said to God: *Father, I praise you for this opportunity to go to Peru and show the people your love and your truth. I praise you for having prepared this team, especially the men. Father, help me to truly seek and revere you. Help me to truly hate sin, and to guard myself that I might not fall to it. Master, you know my heart, you know where I struggle. Give me purity, Daddy, and give me faith and focus for each day and each moment. Show your strength in my weakness, and help me not to get in the way of your message.*

June 20, 2005; Dallas

God led me to pray with DJ . . . and we prayed together that we would hold each other accountable, and truly step up and be the men in the trip that God has called us to be. . . . Afterwards, Walker talked to me and emphasized that he was glad I was here, and really felt that God was going to use me to lead as a man in our group. All in all, God just reaffirmed that I need to take it to the next step as a man in God.

The very first afternoon that I met BJ, we had a wrestling match on the bed. We talked more and more and got to know each other. During worship, I remember we were talking about laying down our childhood.

DJ CONLEY, STUDENT MISSIONARY • PERU 2005

June 21, 2005; Dallas

How God worked in my life today: *We finished drama training and things are going very well.*

The worship service in the evening was even more incredible as God is driving me deeper and deeper into him. For a few years, I have known that a time would come where I would need to humble myself and fall facedown before God so that he could truly

use me. God brought me to that point and showed me that it isn't
because I can, or because I will, or because I am good, but because
he is worthy *that I follow him. Tonight I promised to give him
my life to do with as he pleases because only he is worthy. I gave
my life to obey him instantly. In a sense, I rededicated myself to
him for missions.*

As they had in 2004, the two Awe Star Peru teams traveled
first to Ecuador. BJ continued to reflect on the need to make
his life count.

> *June 22, 2005; Guayaquil, Ecuador*
>
> *What God said to me: The harvest for God's kingdom is ripe
> all around us if we could just learn to see it. "Four months
> until summer," why wait until a mission trip or reaching a certain
> area when there is ministry to be done everywhere?!*
>
> *What I said to God: Father, I just want to praise you for your
> depth, power, authority, love, and worthiness. I thank you for
> allowing me the opportunity to come on this trip and serve, and*

DJ, Logan, and BJ do the *Charlie's
Angels* thing in Ecuador

to just learn about you and seek your face. I am overwhelmed by your depth, but you give me strength and take me deeper. I pray now for focus on you in the following days, and that you would help me to apply what I learn.

From Guayaquil BJ's team traveled to Peru. As they reviewed the drama and prepared to begin ministry, God reminded them that he was the source of their strength. When ministry began, he poured that strength through their lives. Almost immediately, they began to see an amazing harvest.

> *June 24, 2005; Piura, Peru*
> *John 6*
> *What* God said to me: *Often times we are like Andrew and the little boy where a huge task like feeding 12,000 is before us, but all we have is five barley loaves and two fish, a snack for twenty people. We bring our scraps to Jesus; as it says, "Our righteousness is as filthy rags." Yet when we willingly and obediently bring it to Jesus, he makes it work.*

The next few days, everywhere the team went, they saw God "make it work." The evening BJ recorded this journal entry, the group performed the drama at a new site. At first, only a few church members greeted them. Once they began to perform, however, more and more came to watch. After the performance many of them came to Christ.

The next day the team had an even more unusual experience. A huge crowd, including many waiting taxi drivers, gathered to watch them perform. Halfway through the drama, transit cops sent the drivers to move their vehicles. The crowd had grown too large. When the performance was over, the police even told the students to "move on" while they were still leading people to Christ.

Because God was shutting down that site, we knew he had something more for us at another site. As we pulled up to the next spot, we saw that there were many kids from the Piura area there, and they were allowed to come and watch. Right before the drama began, I [David] was called over to talk to a man. We found out that he was from the local news in that area. They wanted an interview and to tape some of the drama. That night the students were seen on the news, performing the drama in the Sechura area.

DAVID POST AND RACHEL BURKHOLDER
AWE STAR MINISTRIES COUNTRY COORDINATORS • PERU 2005

In their POP (Passing on Principles) discipleship sessions, the men of the team had been focusing on God's glory. That emphasis underscored what BJ was learning through *Don't Waste Your Life*. As he had done before, God turned learning into living, with results that could come only through his powerful work.

June 27, 2005; Piura

How God worked in my life today: *God worked in all six drama sites; many came.*

Fifth Drama Site: Before, David taught (no, God taught through Dave) about persecution and opening up. We were truly worshiping and focused on God, and he worked. We were finishing up ministering to a woman, and a group of about seven teenage guys came up and were pointing at [a female team member] . . . and laughing, so I moved between them. Then, I felt God leading me to talk to them, so I did (mucho scardios), but all of them came to Christ.

The God of Abraham, Isaac, and BJ Higgins knew that, although BJ may have been "mucho scardios" (the group of young men was actually a gang, and BJ knew they could easily have responded with violence), he wasn't wasting his life. God was making every moment count by preparing BJ and his team for the greater challenges that lay ahead. BJ's next journal entry describes a critical point:

> June 29, 2005; Piura
> John 11
>
> *W*hat God said to me: *The main theme God showed me was obedience. The disciples had to obey and follow though they were skeptical (v. 16); Mary came immediately when Jesus called her (v. 29); Martha didn't obey Jesus right away, but argued about rolling the stone away. Lazarus, though he was dead, obeyed Jesus and came out (vv. 43–44). If even the dead, wind, and waves obey him immediately, we should also.*
>
> What I said to God: *Help me to be obedient regardless of my feelings. Help me to focus and follow you today.*

BJ's obedience was tested right away. God began to speak to him, not about his service in Peru but about his desires for the following summer.

> June 29, 2005; Piura
>
> *D*ave said, "I'd like to see homeboy go to North Africa." Erin *[Freemyer, Awe Star team director] had also said I should go. . . . In addition, when someone had asked me where I would go if I came back, I heard "North Africa" come out of my mouth before I even thought about it or knew why. First heartbeat, a heartbeat of obedience. Also, Josh's testimony inspired me to go to North Africa and to lay down my life for God.*

As the team prepared to leave Piura, God continued speaking to BJ about his priorities, about the need to avoid wasting his life. Committing to make his life count meant that he must surrender himself and his desires to God. For now, only God knew where this surrender would ultimately lead.

twelve

Heartbeat of Obedience

What God said to me: "Be strong and courageous and do the work. Do not be afraid or discouraged, for the Lord God, my God, is with you. He will not fail or forsake you." Even though many times we are weak and scared, and it seems we have nothing left in us to carry on, and God feels 1,000,000 miles away, the question is not "Do I feel good enough to do this?" or "Am I good enough?" or even "Can I do this?" The answers to these questions are often "no," but God is still with us, and no matter how we feel, the question is *"Will I obey?"*

BJ HIGGINS
PERU JOURNAL • JULY 1, 2004

Follow God.

A heartbeat of obedience was not a new concept for BJ. He had heard Walker Moore teach about it for two summers in a row.

On the 2004 Peru trip, his days had been marked by radical obedience. Even before his Awe Star days, BJ understood a great deal about the importance of listening to God and doing what he said—regardless of where that might take him.

If we would quiet ourselves and listen as it says in Psalm 46:10: "Be still and know that I am God," then we might find God, as Elijah did, in the gentle whisper. . . . God . . . gave Elijah strength and told him to get back in the battle. . . . So quiet your mind, your desires, and turn to God, listening closely, and he will be there for you.

Personal Journal • ca. 2003

In fact, when BJ wrote the "Milk" devotions for Northside's Ultimate Youth Camp in 2003, he emphasized listening to and obeying God.

Read Psalm 95:6–9. Reread verse 8. The Israelites' hearts had been hardened many times while they were wandering in the wilderness. They paid no attention to God and his messengers, and instead followed their own desires. But this only got them into more trouble.

If you turn away from God and harden your hearts, God's patience toward you may wear thin. There will come a day when God has had enough, so be careful not to harden your hearts to him. Pay attention to God and his messengers, or the speakers and leaders, at camp. Make sure that your heart is soft, and your mind is open to whatever God might be trying to tell you. As we approach the end times, it grows more and more important to listen and obey God.

The second year, he was more ready. He had learned more patience. He was also more willing to tell people what he had learned. He wasn't shying away from it. He didn't want to do anything to get in the way of God.

DAVID POST

BJ's passion for serving the Lord and for obedience to the Lord's commands just blew me away from the moment I met him. BJ was an incredible man.

HEATHER SCHAPER, STUDENT MISSIONARY • PERU 2005

As the team continued its progress through Peru, reaching the mountain city of Cajamarca, God urged BJ to instant obedience. His journal entries reflect this significant focus.

July 1, 2005; Cajamarca
John 13
What God said to me: Verses 6–9: Peter understood that Jesus was the Messiah, but he did not understand the idea of service. It's not enough to know about God, you must also know him, follow him, and obey and serve with him.

Mike, BJ, David, DJ, and
Logan in Peru 2005

Verse 10: Jesus has already washed us clean from head to foot. He will never have to do this again, but due to the dirty road of obedience, hardship, and at times, failure, our feet get dirty, so a daily repentance or washing of feet is what we must do. But to get our feet dirty, we must first go.

My prayer for tomorrow is: *obedience and passion, focus and faith.*

The next day, the team was set for the first full day of ministry since reaching Cajamarca. Again, BJ's journal entries center around obedience. Again, God gave him the opportunity to walk out what he had learned, with an awe-inspiring outcome.

July 2, 2005; Cajamarca
John 14

Verses 15–24: Jesus makes a firm connection between obedience and loving him, and between loving him and being loved by God. If we say we follow, believe, and love him, we obey him.

Verses 30–31a: Jesus has all authority.

Verse 31b: Jesus calls us to come follow him and go do his work.

How God worked in my life today: *First drama—rocks. Second drama—prayerwalk plaza. . . . Third—Plaza de Armas again. Had to rely on God's strength to do drama . . . [he had been suffering from diarrhea and vomiting]. At first, one lady went over to Marco (team translator), then God called me to go speak to these four policemen. I [was] kinda nervous because they could've easily laughed in my face or else whipped out their uzis and ordered us to get off the premises, but God is teaching me obedience, so I went and talked to them. As I was speaking, the eyes of two of the four policemen started to well up, and you could tell they wanted Christ. The other two were also sincere. Just as I finished the card [the "911" card that Awe Star students use to share the gospel when no translator is available], Marco walked up. All four of them accepted Christ.*

BJ's boldness in witnessing to the four armed policemen had an immediate impact on his teammates. Even today, when asked about the experiences in Peru that summer, they all recall the day he demonstrated such an incredible heartbeat of obedience.

> After we performed the drama, BJ went and talked to some men, but they were not too receptive, so he felt like he needed to go to the four policemen standing off to the side. My first thought was "What is he doing? He is going to talk to four police officers. They could kick us out!" As usual, BJ was following just what God was saying, and at least two of those police officers prayed and accepted Christ!
>
> MEAGANN EARNHARDT, STUDENT MISSIONARY • PERU 2005

> As we were standing there waiting, BJ started looking around. After a few seconds, he looked at me and said, "I wonder if those gentlemen have been talked to."
> I turned to see who he meant, and was surprised to see him pointing out four policemen! I'll admit that I was a little nervous about talking to guys who could throw us out of the Plaza, but all I said was, "Me . . . too."
> With that, BJ went over to them and explained the gospel. All four of the policemen ended up praying and I know for sure that at least two of them were sincere!! This is just one of the many times that I saw BJ lead someone to the Lord because he was totally obedient to God.
>
> KAYLA TERRALL, STUDENT MISSIONARY • PERU 2005

> I saw the police officers over on the other side of the plaza. I started praying, "Lord, let someone go over and talk to them." Almost immediately, I saw BJ heading their way.
>
> BARBARA ANN SHEELY, STUDENT MISSIONARY • PERU 2005

Satan clearly recognized his foe. The physically small but spiritually mighty person of BJ Higgins was back, and he did not like it at all. Almost immediately BJ became aware of increased attacks on his spirit.

> *July 3, 2005; Cajamarca*
>
> *What I said to God: Father, help me to truly clear the platform of my life and lay down my desires. Help me to be obedient without hesitation and to have the faith like those of Hebrews 11. Continue to break my heart for my team, the Peruvians and for North Africa. Please bring more clarity on this calling. In your Son's name, Amen.*
>
> *Great POP time, then was under attack. Arrived at Plaza de Armas and was still under attack along with a couple others. We prayed and rebuked Satan in God's name and he fled. God showed up and brought a huge crowd and many were saved. I was able to lead one very seeking man to Christ.*

On July 4 Awe Star had planned to give the team a day off. However, God had other plans. Instead of resting, the students took advantage of an opportunity to perform the drama for a school of about three thousand male students. Earlier in the week, a school director's husband had watched the drama. God used him to extend another special invitation. Would they consider performing for a citywide Teacher Recognition Service the next evening?

Awe Star's answer: a heartbeat of obedience. Satan's answer: lies and confusion. Added to this was physical attack. BJ had joked about his digestive problems, speculating that he had picked up a parasite while in Peru in 2004. He even had a name for this unwelcome guest. He called it "Jeff."

BJ never talked about it much, but he was really sick a lot of the time. He said he had a parasite—he even gave it a

124

name—and he was always leaving the dinner table to go to the bathroom. Satan was really attacking us physically. When we performed for the teachers' celebration, sixteen out of the twenty of us were sick.

BARBARA ANN SHEELY

BJ was sick to his stomach almost the whole time. He just never really showed it. He was happy, talking—he was hard-core about the ministry. He had decided to glorify God in his illness.

LOGAN SHIELDS, STUDENT MISSIONARY • PERU 2005

July 5, 2005; Cajamarca

How God worked in my life today: First drama was at a boys' school. I gave testimony. . . . Meanwhile, I finally took Imodium and went on a cracker diet.

Second drama: Unfocused and angry—finally got focused and darkness started to lift just before sword fight. Then, I tripped over a cord as I was going out and though I didn't fall, the music stopped, but we kept going. The climax of my battle was over.

Third drama: We went to the Plaza de Armas for the teacher's convention. +1000 crowd. As we waited for about an hour, Satan started attacking many members of the team physically (illness) or spiritually (distracted). When the time came to do the drama, we rebuked Satan and let God work through us—we had nothing left so we had to rely on him for strength. Through the darkness, his glory shone. We didn't see any salvations, but God showed up. We learned much about glorifying and worshiping and obeying him despite circumstances.

BJ as the Knightmare, Peru 2005

125

The next day the team traveled by bus to Pacasmayo. Within four hours, they made the descent from Cajamarca, at an altitude of ten thousand feet, to Pacasmayo, at sea level just off the Peruvian coast. Although relationship struggles had left them fighting for unity, God had only begun his work through the team of student missionaries.

> *July 10, 2005; Pacasmayo*
> *Genesis 22*
>
> *What God said to me: The incredible faith of Abraham that God would provide, and his unswerving obedience. The trust Isaac had in both God and in Abraham.*
>
> *First Drama: on a plaza on the beach. I gave the Net [Walker Moore's teaching/Awe Star's term for the explanation of the gospel] then was led to talk to three men who wanted to receive Jesus. They came with us to Marco, where a huge crowd gathered, and I got to finish leading them to the Lord and pray with them. Then we went and talked to a Christian from Lima. Also, a group of giggly girls from a school we went to accepted Christ. A group of girls who had seen the drama before at their school accepted Christ at this site.*
>
> *Second drama: Plaza de Armas—We did the drama, though we had been shut down before, and I went to talk and pray with some men. We were then approached by a guy who wanted to practice his English, who then accepted Christ.*

The team's final day in Pacasmayo was just as challenging—and fulfilling—as the others had been. Once again God provided an opportunity to follow him. BJ met that challenge with a heartbeat of obedience.

July 11, 2005; Pacasmayo

*H*ow God worked in my life today: *First drama: school
Second drama: College school—went out and talked to
people. Erin and Dave asked me to talk to the [bus] doorman
when I had been wanting to speak with him for a while. Marco
and I talked to him, and he accepted and prayed and really seemed
to understand quite a bit about the Christian life. At the end, he
gave me a hug.*

BJ let God grow in him in the last year, and over the summer,
you could see it when he talked to people about God. You could
tell that God was speaking through BJ. When he was talking
to people who speak another language, it was amazing to see
him talk about God.

In 2005 he had the opportunity to lead many people to the
Lord. We did not know that he was going to lead the doorman
for one of the buses to Christ, but he did. The first words out
of his mouth when we all got back on the bus were to tell us
about this experience. He was so happy.

SUZANNE ROBERTS, STUDENT MISSIONARY • PERU 2004, 2005

thirteen

Rescue the Perishing

Just as God called Moses to go to Egypt and deliver the Israelites, God called you to go to ALL nations and proclaim the gospel of Jesus Christ in Matthew 28:19, the Great Commission. God wants you—not just preachers and deacons—but you as well to go and tell the world about him. God desires to use you for his glory. When you are out there telling the unsaved, don't worry about the words, for God will give you a passion and the words to say. Let this give you confidence as you approach the world with the gospel of Christ.

BJ HIGGINS
"MILK" DEVOTIONS, 2003

Reach the nations.

As his Awe Star team continued their work in Peru, God continued his work in BJ's heart. The fervor for global missions that the

128

Peru 2004 trip had ignited was rapidly becoming a consuming flame. Its fuel? BJ's growing passion that the nations see and know the glory of God. Awe Star teaches that missions is not an *activity,* but a *lifestyle.* Once again, BJ got it. He really got it.

> I remember one occasion in Peru, when we were at a ministry site, and BJ gave the invitation—the Net. I remember his passion for people and for God could clearly be seen. I've seen many people give the Net, but none of them gave it like BJ did. He had a sincere heart for those people. BJ loved those people. It was a great encouragement to me.
>
> PHILIP TALLMAN

> BJ was a young man who always liked to reflect on things, and he always had questions. I saw in him a huge passion that people would come to know Jesus, and he was always looking for people that no one had shared with so that he could approach them and share with them.
>
> PASTOR TITO SEVILLA • TRUJILLO, PERU

> BJ would always be reading in his Bible or journaling when he was given even five minutes of "free time." He wanted to make sure that he was always ready for that one opportunity to share the love of Christ with the lost people around him. When he shared his testimony or talked about the things of God, he had a different tone of voice that he used—one filled with love, compassion, and urgency. After all, tomorrow could be too late for that one person out there listening.
>
> ASHLEY REAGAN, STUDENT MISSIONARY • PERU 2004

> I saw this little guy who was questioning God and pursuing him changing to somebody that was realizing that God had fashioned him as a tool for kingdom purposes. He was really beginning to see that in a very concrete way. His first mission trip sank the nations in on his heart. I think it really began to

knit into him a passion for reaching others in other parts of the world. He may have heard about reaching the nations from somebody else before, but it's totally different when you experience it yourself.

He was obviously changed from the first time that he went to Peru. I think it's a real lesson to so many of us, that a young man even as young as he was could do so much. I think we should expect more out of our kids. They have an amazing way of demonstrating to us that God can do amazing things. I think that now BJ had tasted something that I think he had wanted to taste—it was obviously within him, deeply set within his heart very quickly.

I was used to seeing that as a youth pastor. It's just an amazing thing when you put kids in a different culture: they see the world through a different lens, see God through the eyes of another person. It changes their perspective on life. Not only did that happen for BJ, something clicked inside his spirit. He really began to understand something about how he was made and what he was made for.

Uncle Rich

July 12, 2005; Trujillo, Peru
Psalm 105

What God said to me: *Verses 1–3: Tell others about him. Verse 4: Search for the Lord and his strength.*
Verses 9–44: The story of Israel from Abraham to Joshua, pulling it all together and revealing its common theme and purpose as another puzzle piece of God's story; God's glory.
Verse 45: It was all so that they would obey and glorify God.

God continued to prepare BJ's spirit for all that he would live out over the next days and weeks. No one could have known the level of obedience that God would ultimately call forth—or the glory he would receive as a result.

July 13, 2005; Trujillo

*H*ow God worked in my life today: *Fifth drama: Street by large plaza. Huge crowd gathered. My group talked to a large group of women and led them to Christ, then another small group, despite distractions. We were very focused today, more so than we had been for several weeks. Every site brought glory to God and was rewarding, even though we only ministered twice.*

My prayer for tomorrow is: *That we would be even more focused and only talk of the things of God and seek his glory to shine on our drama sites.*

The team continued ministering in Trujillo, seeking out and drawing the people of Peru toward the glory of God.

July 14, 2005; Trujillo

Isaiah 66: verse 14b–15a, 18b, 19c: God proclaims his name and destroys his enemies to bring him glory.

July 15, 2005; Trujillo

*H*ow God worked in my life today: *Fifth drama: After the drama (I gave introduction and testimony), Dave told me to take Marco and go talk to the [school] Director, so I did. As I was talking, his face was very intense and his eyes were welling up. As he prayed, I couldn't help but smile as several of the kids around him who had been listening prayed as well.*

Sixth drama: Plaza de Armas. Before, our team earnestly prayed, and prayed, and cried out to God during the twenty–thirty minutes on the bus ride before the site. We set up, and the guard, who should have kicked us out (main square of largest city in Peru) allowed us twenty minutes. God gathered many seeking souls, and the guard himself accepted Christ.

As they prepared to leave Trujillo for their return to Ecuador and the United States, the team began to recognize that their ministry could continue. God again revealed his desire that the nations know and worship him.

July 17, 2005; Trujillo and Piura

How God worked in my life today: *After going to church with Tito, we went out and did a drama in the street. I was a POL ("people of the land")—one who accepted Christ. [Awe Star sometimes has the students change roles to help them focus]. I had a blast and really worshiped. We then went and talked to two girls who then accepted Christ.*

The second drama was again in the Plaza de Armas, and I (and the team) was equally focused, but through worship and fellowship instead. We went up to two different groups of ladies, and both walked away. Then we went to a large group of ladies who, while we were witnessing, understood so much that we thought they might be saved already, but they were just seeking God that much! We prayed with them, then more and more people kept coming up and praying with Lucho (translator). Meanwhile, I got to witness to and pray with our doorman.

Afterwards, since I couldn't find a hard case for our guitar to take back to the states, I offered it to David (Peruvian). Turns out that

it has been a lifetime dream of his to have his own instrument, because he loves music and plays guitar, piano, and percussion. Daniel, Tito's son, gave me a goodbye hug twice at the bus station.

BJ leads worship for Peru 2005

I get excited when I see the guitar that BJ gave to a seminary student [David] that continues to be used to win souls and lead believers to worship the Lord. In my life it is a huge inspiration to continue to do ministry.

PASTOR TITO SEVILLA

July 18, 2005; Piura and Guayaquil

*H*ow God worked in my life today: *Person was twenty-five minutes early in bus seat—Logan's seat, though we had it booked. I gave him a tract, then shared Christ with him. Marco was in the seat right in front of us, so he translated. Martin said he wanted to change his life and accept Jesus (stop drinking, partying). We prayed with him, gave him my last booklet, and talked to him about the Christian life. . . . Since I got my new Gideon Spanish-English Bible, I gave him my old Spanish Bible.*

While Beej was in Peru this year, he was very excited to find a Bible that was a parallel English and Spanish version. As he relayed the story, he said, "I was in this hotel, and they had this English/Spanish Bible in the room. You know the Gideons put those there so you can take them, so I did!"

"BJ," I said, "the Gideons don't put those there so you can take them. They put them there so that they will be available in the room for unbelievers and believers alike."

"They do?" he said. Then he quickly justified the whole experience by saying, "It's okay. I gave my old Spanish Bible to someone in Peru."

It is fitting that many have opted to donate money to the Gideons. Hopefully, a new Spanish/English Bible will find its way into that hotel room. (A Gideon or two has since told me that BJ was closer to right than I was. He would love that, and not let me forget it.)

Dad, blog posting
October 20, 2005

July 19, 2005; Guayaquil
Matthew 9:33–38

What God said to me: *Verse 37: Jesus called all of us to work, to be world Christians, not just a few. God wants all of his children to respond to the call.*

Verse 38: World Christian habit: Prayer. When we pray, we must ask and seek God earnestly and pray for his glory to shine more.

Heather, BJ, Kayla, Brooke, and Mary, Peru 2005

After flying out of Ecuador, the team arrived at debriefing in Dallas, eager to rejoin friends from other Awe Star teams and then return home. In both Texas and Indiana, BJ eagerly shared his stories from Peru. Perhaps even more, he longed to share his passion for reaching the world. As he had written in June, God had already begun the process of calling him for the next summer. This time, he believed God wanted him in North Africa.

BJ sounded different than he did in 2004—his testimonies were not so rehearsed-sounding but much more natural. He kept going right into the stories, right into the heart of the matter. It was as if he knew what we wanted to hear. I remember being so excited! I loved it when he spoke in front of our church. He was so eloquent. He really captured some of the main things that had happened.

Mom

He was on fire for God. He took every chance he could to share about his experiences. It seemed to me like he was ready to lead the next big Christian uprising.

TAYLOR DEBAUN

When he would talk, he talked with a lot more passion. He talked like he was talking to hundreds of people at once, even if he was just talking to you one-on-one. He just made sure, or tried to make sure, that everyone had that same passion.

JACK MEILS

During the first week of August, BJ sent an email to his Awe Star teammates that communicated much of his heart and passion for reaching the nations.

Hey Family!
I echo each of you in that I am totally missing all of you and our accountability and companionship.

Well, since I got back, God has given me the opportunity to share mainly with my family and our summer missionaries, of whom two or three are seriously considering going on a trip with Awe Star next year. Also, my dad will hopefully be able to go to the Mexico trip this winter, so if you guys could be praying for that, I would appreciate it.

Friday I spent the night sharing stories with my family and some with the summer missionaries who are staying at our camp. On Saturday, I bought a new guitar, which I used in worship on Sunday. I was also invited to speak to my church on the things God had done, which was cool.

Like I'm sure you all are experiencing, there was so much that I wanted to say to challenge my church as well as tell the stories of Peruvians coming to Christ, but I wasn't sure if I got my message across. But then a man came up to me afterwards talking about how he really felt challenged and how we as Christians need to get busy serving God, so I was totally praising God that he spoke to at least one person.

Tonight I was able to [share with the summer missionaries serving at Highland Lakes Camp] about what God has been teaching me as well as tell them even more stories of Peruvian salvations. . . . Wednesday night I will be going to my friend's youth group . . . which will probably ask me to share, since they did last year, so I'm excited about that.

I love each and every one of you and I really miss you guys. I am praying for you. Keep in touch.

In Christ's love, BJ

LETTER TO AWE STAR TEAMMATES, JULY 2005

I asked him if he'd like to share something in the service. He did, and I wish we had recorded it. He did a fabulous job. It was very well put together, not just "I did this," "I saw this," "I went here." It was not just a report; it was a report challenge, a strong challenge to the entire church to consider what you're going to do with your life.

PASTOR LARRY FLOYD

I knew that God was going to use BJ. He talked like he was preaching to the masses. I could see him as a pastor one day. When he got back, I saw that he cared for the people in Peru, but not just for what it did for him. Many people think, *I'm a good Christian; I should go on a mission trip.* BJ taught me about the true passion he had for the people of Peru.

LAUREN

The fire within BJ was obvious: to the people of Peru, to his Awe Star teammates, to his family, to his pastor, and to his friends. BJ had begun to catch the concept of being a "world Christian," someone who shares Christ's burden for a world dying without him. He ached for the people of Peru. He longed to go to North Africa to share with the people there. He was committed to reaching the nations with the gospel of Christ. As his focus sharpened, his vision expanded.

As always, BJ found music that reflected the cry of his heart. Christian recording artists Billy and Cindy Foote introduced their music to the student missionaries during ASU. When he returned home, BJ could not wait to share this song with his family. He played it again and again, at full volume every time. The lyrics echo his burden to reach the nations—as well as the vision that had already begun shaping his legacy.

Rescue the Perishing

Rescue the perishing
Care for the dying
Snatch them in pity
From sin and the grave
Weep o'er the erring one
Lift up the fallen one
Tell them of Jesus
The mighty to save

Chorus:
Rescue the perishing
Care for the dying
Jesus is merciful
Jesus will save
Church open your eyes once more
And see what Christ died for
Jesus is merciful
Jesus will save

Down in the human heart
Crushed by the tempter
Feelings lie buried
That grace can restore
Touched by a loving heart
Wakened by kindness

Chords that are broken
Will vibrate once more

Chorus

Bridge:
As we're playing our songs
While we're singing them well
Have we forgotten the lost
The reality of hell
If we wanna serve God
Wanna see his will done
Do we offer our lives
Or just the songs we have sung?

Do we even care?
When will we care?

To rescue the perishing
Care for the dying
Jesus is merciful
Jesus will save

Church open your eyes once more
And see what Christ died for
Jesus is merciful
Jesus will save

BILLY JAMES FOOTE, FANNY JANE CROSBY

Section Five

The Battle

Do you not know? Have you not heard? The LORD is the everlasting God, the Creator of the ends of the earth. He will not grow tired or weary, and his understanding no one can fathom. He gives strength to the weary and increases the power of the weak. Even youths grow tired and weary, and young men stumble and fall; but those who hope in the LORD will renew their strength. They will soar on wings like eagles; they will run and not grow weary, they will walk and not be faint.

ISAIAH 40:28–31 (NIV)

fourteen

Daily Christian Dying

"Daily Christian living is daily Christian dying." . . . How often do we live like our own lives are so important, like all of our comforts, friends, and circumstances are the greatest things ever, and yet Christ clearly says "Whoever holds on to his life will lose it, but whoever gives up his life for me will gain it back" (Mark 8:35). And then again in John 12:25 he says that he who loves his life will lose it. Then [John] Piper says [in *Don't Waste Your Life*], "These may be taken from us at any time in the path of Christ-exalting obedience. . . ."

So we die to ourselves and lay down our lives daily so that we will be ready when our lives, our comfort, our family, wealth, or friends are taken from us in our walk with Christ.

BJ HIGGINS
WWW.XANGA.COM/DEADSILENCE7 • AUGUST 2, 2005

Die to self daily.

BJ got it. He really got it. Brent Allen Higgins Jr. would do whatever it took to serve his Master. Ultimately, this meant that like

141

the apostle Paul, he had to die to himself and his own desires—to consider others as more important than himself, and to surrender his own wants or wishes to the greater cause of Christ. While still in Peru, he had posted this on his Xanga weblog:

So far the main thing God has been teaching me is obedience, and IMMEDIATE obedience to him.

JULY 12, 2005

Exactly what did that obedience mean? On the mission field, it meant consistently seeking out the lost. It meant being the last one to come in from a time of witnessing after the drama presentation. On the flight back to Indiana, it meant making sure that his seatmate heard "how Christ is the meaning and should be the center of all life." At church, it meant sharing about his Peru trip—and his vision for future ministry—with anyone who would stop and listen. At home, it meant talking to his family about his heart for the nations. It meant leading a friend to Christ via instant messaging (see the entire text of the IM witnessing experience at the end of this book). It meant laying down his rights in favor of relationships—in other words, dying to self day after day after day.

How often do we really live as Christ? How often do we lay our own dreams and wants down for God? At church camp? On mission trips? Maybe even every Sunday or Wednesday? But Christ says DAILY. Too often do we attempt the whole "Christian living" on Sundays and Wednesdays, and forget the whole "DAILY Christian dying." Christ calls us to die daily.

WWW.XANGA.COM/DEADSILENCE7 • AUGUST 2, 2005

BJ was always excited about ministry. When we went out to witness after drama performances, he was always the last one back. He was always looking for more people, talking to the security guard or the doorman. That was an everyday thing for him. He had no fear; he was so unselfish, so compelled by the love of the Lord. He was like, "They're lost, they're dying, and we have to do something about it!"

KRISTIN DUTT, STUDENT MISSIONARY • PERU 2005

He kept talking about North Africa. "Oh, you're gonna come too; only maybe you don't know it yet," he told me.

LAUREN

I got to see BJ and talk with him a little bit after his return from Peru. I would have expected him to be just overflowing with stories of the mission trip he had just completed, or maybe even basking in the glory of what he had just accomplished. His total focus on where God was leading him was kind of amazing to me. All he wanted to talk about was where God was leading him next, which was to Africa. There was a very strong conviction in his heart—North Africa was where he needed to go.

GLEN CHRISTIE, FAMILY FRIEND

God was clearly at work. But as BJ had discovered in Peru, the Enemy watches that work and seeks to destroy it in every way he can. BJ had arrived at the Awe Star debriefing with some mild signs of illness. Walker Moore remembers asking him about his health. "Just a cold," BJ told him—nothing unusual, considering the long hours of traveling and the climate changes. Back at home, he had a similar answer for Mom when she mentioned his occasional diarrhea: "It's no big deal."

*Y*ou see, as Christians we are to give our lives up every day, to die to ourselves every day, to let go of all of our attachments and affections and be willing to let go of life itself everyday because we treasure Christ higher than life.

So often, we get preoccupied and distracted with all of the little details of life and all of our wants and dreams and desires, and yet as Paul says in Philippians "To live is Christ." All of the details don't matter, all of our wants and dreams are of no consequence because our lives, as Christians, are to be for Christ and Christ alone.

WWW.XANGA.COM/DEADSILENCE7 • AUGUST 2, 2005

BJ told me, "I love how Piper says what he thinks 'to live is Christ and to die is gain' means." I told him, "I just never really get it." BJ said, "Well, let's talk about it," and we did. He told me it meant to live out our lives as Christ did, that sometimes it would mean suffering, or just being willing to lay down our own desires. When we die like this, there will always be gain.

DJ CONLEY • PERU 2005

BJ had learned to die to self by letting go of daily distractions. However, the lump that appeared under his right arm two weeks after he returned was more than a distraction. He told us that it kept him from raising his arm much above his head.

We had not yet connected with a doctor in our new community, so Mom took BJ to a nearby clinic. The physician who examined him seemed only mildly concerned. "It's soft. That's a good sign. Probably just a swollen lymph node," he said, prescribing an antibiotic and a return visit in a week.

After a week, nothing had changed. Was it a cyst? The clinic doctor suggested an appointment with a surgeon, who could do more testing. Mom scheduled the appointment. Just after that, BJ reported that the antibiotic had finally done its job. The troublesome lump had shrunk to almost nothing. Relieved, we decided to postpone the appointment until after our planned trip to Gatlinburg, Tennessee—our first family vacation in years. Only Whitney, about to begin her freshman year of college as a nursing major, had to remain behind for several required orientation sessions.

The weekend before the trip, Lauren and her younger brother attended Northside's Jump Start, a back-to-school youth event designed to help students refocus spiritually.

I was a youth intern at Northside that summer, and this would be the last event of my time there. BJ and I spent some great time together that weekend. On Sunday we went to the zoo in St. Louis. That was right about the time that he started feeling sick—I even remember teasing him about it.

Lauren

This was the first time I'd seen him since he got back from Peru. I'd heard him talking to other people, and there was definitely something different about him—you could just tell. For the hour we were on the bus, there was no holding him back. He absolutely told me that I needed to be a missionary. It was like he knew my calling. The Holy Spirit was obviously speaking through him.

Eric David, family friend and student missionary • Chile 2005

At the end of the weekend, we prepared to leave for Tennessee. BJ seemed tired and out of sorts. We knew he didn't really want to go along, although (for once) he didn't say very much. Dad, veteran of many Jump Start retreats, knew that BJ had probably lost some sleep during the time spent there. He could catch up in the car.

Gatlinburg was a time of contrasts: Relaxing hours spent playing games or reading in our rented cabin. A thread of concern over the cough that BJ couldn't seem to shake. Dinners out, laughing, and talking. Moments of frustration, even argument, with a BJ who seemed (far too often, as we saw it) "too tired" to join us. A challenging hike on a mountain trail, one of our favorite ways of spending time together. An unusually quiet BJ, who slept nearly all the way home. He had done his best to participate. He could push his body only so far.

Lauren and BJ in Gatlinburg

John 12

Verses 24–25: We must die to ourselves and become empty so that Christ can grow and bear fruit through us.

Verse 26: If you want to become a disciple of Christ, you must actively get up, obey the call, come, and follow him. If you want to be great or a leader, you must be a servant (Matt. 20:26–28). If you want to be a servant, you must be where Christ is. . . . Belief is only halfway; you must also obey.

PERU JOURNAL • JUNE 30, 2005

BJ in Gatlinburg the week before going into the hospital

> Even though BJ was feeling so bad, we got some of the best pictures of him that we had ever taken. His smile was incredible! By the end of the week, it was obvious that he was getting worse. As we packed the car to return home, I had a moment of premonition. Although I didn't make the connection with BJ's illness, I had the distinct impression that this was the last time we would do something together as a family.
>
> Dad

When we reached home Friday night, August 12, there was no doubt about it. BJ was seriously ill. Feverish, he spent a restless night. The next morning, we drove him to a Prompt Care clinic. There, the doctor diagnosed the problem as walking pneumonia. She prescribed a stronger antibiotic, saying that BJ just needed some time. We both stayed home from church Sunday to care for him. He was sleeping very little and eating almost nothing.

The following day Mom woke early for the first day of her new school year. Although we had moved, she continued teaching at Pleasant View Elementary in Zionsville, forty-five minutes away. BJ told her that he felt better, encouraging her to go to school as planned. Once again, he was living out what he believed: we must die to self by considering the needs of others more important than our own.

To love is to care about and dwell on others, not one's self. That thing that you think about most, write about most, talk about most is what you have centered your life on. We must be careful not to become self-centered, nor centered on any other than God. Even when we treat others with love, it should always be ultimately for God and centered around him, lest we become obsessed or idolize some person. Today/tomorrow, think about how many times you think about, complain, or comment about your conditions or situations, and make an effort to focus, instead, on God and loving others. Love is not self-centered.

FROM A LETTER TO A FRIEND • 2004

Mom went on to school. Her prayers and concern for BJ weighed heavily on her heart. As Dad recalls, the morning passed in a haze. His lack of sleep matched BJ's, and he never even considered going to work. Father and son spent long hours waiting for a return call from our former family doctor. Finally, BJ could wait no longer. "Dad, can we just go to the emergency room?" The two headed out for the thirty-minute drive.

When they arrived at the hospital, Dad hurried toward the emergency room doors. BJ's feeble voice stopped him midstride: "Dad, could you slow down? I can't keep up." He leaned heavily on his father as they made their way into the hospital.

From that point on, everything seemed to accelerate. Blood tests showed a white cell count five times higher than normal. X-ray results proved equally alarming. Before long, a doctor came into the curtained examination area, his expression quietly urgent. "Mr. Higgins, I have to inform you that your son is extremely ill."

"I know," Dad responded dully. "That's why we're here."

The doctor gazed straight into Dad's eyes as if to underscore his next words. "You don't understand. Your son is among the top 2 percent of critically ill people in the world. As a matter of fact, I need to transport him to a hospital with a pediatric ICU, as he is likely to end up on a ventilator."

The words reached Dad through a thick fog of disbelief. Somehow, his mind stumbled through the list of hospital possibilities that the doctor handed him and chose the one—St. Vincent's in Indianapolis—that was closest to Mom's school. As soon as the doctor left the room, Dad reached for his cell phone, anxious to give his wife the latest update. BJ's rasping voice broke into his urgency: "Dad, I know you're scared. I believe the Lord will deliver me through this. But if he doesn't, I'm going home to be with him, and that's okay with me."

Before long the two shared another ride—in an ambulance. With BJ and an attendant in the back, Dad rode shotgun beside the driver, who fought traffic most of the way into the city. BJ lay quietly except for his nearly constant coughing.

An anxious Mom arrived at the hospital ahead of the ambulance. Our pastor, Larry Floyd, was already waiting. He had hurried to St. Vincent's after receiving a phone call from Mom's close friend Carol Jones.

> We had already been praying, because we knew BJ didn't seem to be getting any better. That morning, Deanna called here at home and said that Brent had taken him to the emergency room. It seemed like hardly any time later, maybe only an hour, when she called again. She was very upset and in tears, telling us, "They're sending him to St. Vincent's. They're taking him by ambulance."
>
> CAROL JONES

> I had no clue as to the severity of the problem, and neither did Deanna. When BJ came in, I got to see him and talk to him just briefly. I had prayer there with Brent and Deanna. I told them, "You should go home tonight; he's going to be fine."
> He wasn't fine.
>
> PASTOR LARRY FLOYD

Barely able to breathe, much less speak, BJ once again showed his commitment to die to self as the staff took him through the admissions procedures. When his sister Lauren arrived, he began telling her about his concern that Dad, who had spent so much time with him during the past few days, might catch "whatever it is I have."

149

By this time the intensive care doctor had seen his X-ray. The near whiteout of BJ's lungs indicated massive infection. The pediatric ICU's newest patient would be placed in isolation until tests could determine exactly why he had become so ill.

> His concern for his dad was evident in the sound of his voice, and it was much greater than the concern he had for his own life at this time. My time with the rest of the family was short on this admission day, as I had to give a report to the night shift that were beginning to arrive. BJ was going to be staffed "one-on-one" that night. His X-ray, labs, and overall condition gave every indication that he was about to become critical in the upcoming hours.
>
> DONNA GUIDER, RN

BJ's small steps of obedience, his daily dying to self, had prepared him for the next step—the greater step. As the vigil began, no one knew how many others would soon share in his journey.

fifteen

So the World Will See

Jesus prayed that we would be filled with joy, protected from evil, made pure and holy, taught in the truth and made entirely God's. What stood out to me the most is how Jesus prayed over and over for our protection and sanctification, but mostly, our unity as the body of Christ.

BJ HIGGINS
PERU JOURNAL • JULY 5, 2005

Pursue unity among believers.

The unity of the body of Christ. BJ had long understood its importance. He talked, prayed, and of course, wrote about the need for unity among believers—even when he was only nine years old:

Acts 6–8; 1 Timothy 3:9

Y *ou should solve the problem rather than cause the problem. There is no perfect church.*

To elect a new pastor won't make a perfect church. To elect new deacons won't make a perfect church, to get more staff or do more programs won't make a perfect church. Summary: nothing will make a perfect church because a church is made by human beings.

Satan will try to create a problem in the church, but the church should be too strong and too spiritual so that Satan can't turn the focus of the church from missions to the problem.

PERSONAL JOURNAL • DECEMBER 27, 1998

Family and friends agree. BJ longed for church unity. Once again, he did much more than talk about it. He lived it. BJ's authentic love for people showed in nearly everything he did. In virtually any situation, his encouraging words, his unselfish actions, and even his teasing helped involve and unite others.

We had a relationship of mutual encouragement; he was never condemning. Even when he confronted someone, he did it in a loving way.

JACK MEILS

One night on our mission trip to Corbin, we looked out and saw several picnic tables. Some of our kids were at one table, and—a couple tables over—there were a few more of our kids. One of our leadership team told us, "They're feuding"—just a typical teenage argument.

After supper the kids had dispersed, and we said, "We're not going to let this continue." Right then, that same leadership team member came up and said, "Forget the problem with the kids. BJ took care of it." He just sat down with them and said, "This is not right," and showed them in Scripture why they needed to be in unity. That spoke volumes as to what he was all about.

LOWELL JONES

I think his encouragement to individuals really helped us grow together in unity. He was very caring. He would encourage people and help them on a day-to-day basis.

LAURA OKSOL, STUDENT MISSIONARY • PERU 2004, 2005

BJ was a man of God, but he was fun to be around. There's a picture of him peeking out from a hammock in Guayaquil. That was BJ, doing things like that just to make people laugh. He really helped bring the group together.

BJ wrapped in a hammock

DAVID POST

St. Vincent's pediatric ICU staff acted quickly. The decision to place BJ in isolation meant that anyone who entered his room had to be completely gloved, gowned, and masked. Everything he had brought with him—including a well-loved, tattered Bible—was removed from the room and destroyed.

The first night BJ (visible through the glass that made up one wall of his room) could wave at visiting friends. Within the next twenty-four hours, doctors made the decision to increase his medication level, sedating him. It became obvious that they suspected something very serious—and that BJ's life hung in the balance.

His voice silenced by the ventilator, his awareness blocked by the powerful drugs, BJ lay as if in a coma. Despite the Enemy's obvious influence, God was already at work to unite believers through our son's illness. In fact, three church families—Northside in Indianapolis, Crosswinds in Carmel, and First Baptist in Mooresville—worked together to minister to us. They brought us food, visited, and (most important of all) mobilized others to pray. Back in Tulsa, the Awe Star family also began assembling its forces for prayer.

Acts: a great example of the perfect church—in complete unity, sharing everything, seeking your possessions to give to the needy. We need to be just like that, yet we become so materialistic, let little things get between us, and argue over everything. We need to be like the believers in this passage. . . . Father, I pray that our team, our churches, and our brothers and sisters in you would become more like that body of believers, and that you would take away our materialism and pettiness.

PERU JOURNAL • JUNE 28, 2004

I was taking a team to New York City for a mission trip with Upward Basketball. When we heard that BJ was in the hospital, our mission team began to pray. I remember saying, "Lord, this is going to be one of the longest weeks of my ministry. I want to go home and be with my family and the Higgins family." I called the Upward people, and immediately they began praying all across the country for BJ.

PASTOR RUSTY KENNEDY

Although the Higgins family had not lived in the area very long, they became a real part of the church family simply because of the kind of people they are. They took a large part in the praise ministry and our small groups. When BJ got sick, we were pretty heavily invested in ministering to them.

PASTOR LARRY FLOYD

> Pastor Bill Chaulk of Crosswinds Community really flew under the radar. He and his wife Karen were there constantly to support and encourage us. They would show up in their motorcycle leathers. Usually they would find a time to come when nobody else was there.
>
> Hearing that man pray for BJ was like hearing no one else in my life pray. The Lord was uniquely present in the time we shared together. When other people showed up, he was quick to bow out.
>
> Dad

When Brent called, we already knew that we would do everything we could to stand shoulder-to-shoulder with the Higgins family. The message went out that very day on cell phones, text messages, email, however we could send it.

WALKER MOORE

We were watching BJ's prayers for unity realized as the body of Christ worked together by praying, visiting, and providing meals. From the first day of BJ's hospitalization, we never had to think about food. Between our friends from all three churches and the hospital staff, who gave us frequent vouchers for the hospital cafeteria, our meals were provided every day.

Food. Such a minor need compared to a much more critical issue: what was wrong with BJ? Dad called Awe Star right away to check on other student missionaries. Doctors' questions kept returning to BJ's recent trip to Peru. Had anyone traveling with him become ill?

The answer was no. None of his family members, friends, Awe Star teammates, or anyone else with whom he had come in contact ever became even slightly ill. So what was wrong with BJ?

The Battle

My brother is a doctor, and with other doctors here, they did a report on common sicknesses that were going around Peru, and they sent it to the doctor that was helping BJ.

PASTOR TITO SEVILLA

[Doctors] did not immediately share with us their belief. Still, we had to ... [wear] protective garb ... to protect ourselves and others. ... The interesting thing was that we did not know for a while the reasons for such caution.

Dad, blog posting
March 7, 2007

As doctors explored more possibilities, the body of Christ came together in prayer. The love shown to BJ and his family was something he understood well. In fact, in 2004 he had written about it in a letter to a friend:

Christ said, "You can recognize my followers by their love for each other." You see, we live in a non-loving world, so to love is to stick out, be different, go against the flow. What is it that 90 to 100 percent of the time brings people to Christ? Love. God's love is something that this unloving world has never seen before. Our biggest witness should be our love—the reflecting of God's love (2 Corinthians 3:18).

A mysterious infection. Bulky machines. Miles of tubing. Potent medications. These combined to place a rare barrier between the family and BJ, one that we were determined to break in any way we could. Even with the extra precautions that his isolation required, we all spent much of our time beside him. We stroked his hair; we sang to him; we read Scripture aloud. Contemporary Christian CDs, particularly his favorite songs from Billy and Cindy Foote or MercyMe (and, when the medical team would tolerate it, his favorite metal core band, Haste the Day) played almost constantly from a boom box a nurse had produced from somewhere.

When we left BJ's room, we often talked and prayed in the small waiting room nearby. At first, our many visitors kept this area so full that friends mistakenly assumed it was a private reception area. We used a nearby "parent room" for needed moments alone.

That first Wednesday night, two important events occurred. Earlier, doctors had explained to us that the ventilator alone could not meet BJ's needs. They recommended treatment with an ECMO (extracorporeal membrane oxygenation) machine designed to recirculate both blood and oxygen, bypassing the lungs and lessening the strain on the heart. With ECMO the doctors said BJ's chances of survival were 40–50 percent. Without it—no one wanted to ask. Again BJ's own words, written in 2004, describe the situation best.

Psalm 118:5–9: When I am in trouble or hopeless or in dire circumstances, I can take hope in God, for he is sovereign and he can and will rescue me. I can trust him, and trust him only. . . . For the past week, we have been praying for unity. . . . If we have done/do anything right, [it is that] we did/do pray together as a group.

PERU JOURNAL • JUNE 26, 2004

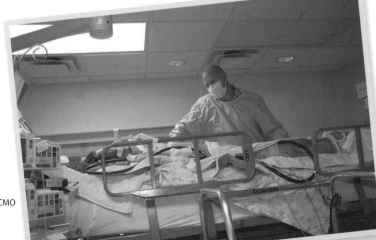

BJ on ECMO

The ECMO treatment meant that BJ had to be moved to a much larger room, crowded with exchange and surgical equipment. The decision was made. The time for the complex transfer was set for that night.

Not long before the procedure began, a sudden influx of visitors shocked us. The reception area overflowed. The hallways filled with friends, all intent on supporting BJ. Dad, helpless in both his concern for our son and his inability to deal with the crush of people, suggested the only possible solution: "Let's pray." The body of Christ joined him as he dropped to his knees.

I just remember Brent coming out into the hallway where people were waiting. At first, he started to talk and was just weeping. Then everyone got down on the floor and started to pray for BJ. I had taken Deanna back to the family area at that time to have some privacy.

My husband, Lowell, told me that Brent prayed, "Lord, he's in your hands. You gave him to me, and he's yours, not mine—he's never been mine. I will give you the glory no matter how you choose to work in this." It was just one of those jaw-dropping experiences.

CAROL JONES

It was just amazing to me how many people were there. For me, the experience started changing right then. Initially, it was my nephew who was in the hospital. I knew it was serious. I had been in the meeting with Brent and Deanna and the doctors. Somehow, seeing that level of support made me realize that there was something going on that was beyond ordinary. At that point, I couldn't have told you what it was, but it made me realize that this was not a typical illness and not a typical situation.

As more and more people prayed, I couldn't help but think, *They're going to come and tell us to leave. They're going to tell us to break this up.* That never happened. I never became aware of anyone coming or going, and I don't know how they could have gotten by all of us anyway. I just was absolutely amazed.

UNCLE BRAD

BJ slept on in isolation, unaware of the kneeling crowd filling the hallways and reception areas. His heart cry, expressed the previous summer, was being realized: "*What God said to me*: Message on mind and heart for unity and love in the church."

Pastor Rusty Kennedy wanted those who were praying to be able to get updates without bothering the family. He contacted other men from Northside, asking them to help him set up a website to serve this purpose. One even donated a laptop computer for us to use. Rusty's most difficult task was convincing us, especially Mom, of the wisdom of this approach.

Deanna was against the blog at first. She felt that it was going to be an invasion of their privacy. It really ended up being a huge blessing to all of them.

CAROL JONES

The team of men came up with a weblog format to allow for postings both from the family and from BJ's prayer partners. They used some Xanga blogs that Lauren had posted about her brother's situation as opening entries for the new site. The word dispersed quickly: check www.prayforbj.com rather than calling or going to the hospital.

We tried to be very balanced in how we helped them. Early on, Brent and Deanna were overwhelmed with so many people coming and wanting to help. We made it very clear to our people: don't come unless we ask you to.

PASTOR LARRY FLOYD

The Battle

As BJ continued his life-and-death battle, the blog allowed us to regain some control. The very first comments displayed the unity that both Jesus and BJ prized—a unity that would sustain and support us through the difficult days ahead. BJ's relentless pursuit of unity among believers was bearing fruit all around us. God alone knew exactly how far—and how soon—that unity would extend.

In John 17, Jesus prays for us that we might be united together and in him so the world will see we are from God.

PERU JOURNAL • JULY 5, 2005

This message is spreading through email like wildfire! Everyone who gets it passes it on to all their email pals, so it is unimaginable all the prayer support BJ will receive.

BLOG POSTING

I remember talking to Brent, because the first couple of days, Deanna was going crazy with the phone calls. I remembered that someone else who had a child who was ill for an extended time had started a website. I remember suggesting it to Brent, and I guess at the same time, somebody was coming up with the idea for the blog.

DONNA GUIDER

Dear Jesus, you created BJ. You hold him in your loving arms. You have given him an awesome understanding of you and your Word. You know he is a gift to all of us. You have given him your love for all people. You know his desire for the unity of your people. You are receiving glory through his illness. Now with countless others, I ask you to bring healing to his body. Guide the medical staff during these new surgical procedures. . . . Bless all his family, and give them added strength we pray. In your precious name. Amen.

AUNT LISA TEEGARDEN, BLOG POSTING • AUGUST 31, 2005

sixteen

www.prayforbj.com

God will ALWAYS be here, even though WE will not. EVERY-THING else will fade and fall in this world (meaning the physical world, because I know that my spirit and soul will live forever), but GOD will not. I will never have to rely on myself, although I have tried before, and every time I did, I fell and failed. Never will the day come that I will have to rely on myself, and never will the day come that God won't exist.

BJ HIGGINS
HTTP://THENO1HANGOUT.PROBOARDS3.COM • MAY 20, 2004

Trust in a faithful God.

The faithful God whom BJ's family and friends turned to in our time of need was the faithful God BJ served. For most of his fifteen years, he had boldly pointed people toward that God, encouraging them to do as he did—entrust God with everything they had.

Our reliance on God had built this radical faith into BJ's life from his earliest days. As he grew, he began to embrace it as his own. In a journal entry, he shared some of his struggles:

After my fifth-grade year of school ended . . . I watched a television program that faced me with sudden anxieties and realizations that threw me into a state of constant worry. I was constantly worrying with nothing to worry about, constantly scared with nothing to be afraid of. I was depressed, sick of worrying, tired of being scared. It was tearing me apart from the inside. I was sick to my stomach, I was always tired, but it wasn't very noticeable from the outside. After much prayer, God pulled me out of this rut just in time for school. After this, I realized what God was trying to teach me: trust him and don't worry.

PERSONAL JOURNAL • MARCH 9, 2002

BJ learned his lesson well. His very next journal entry reads:

Have faith in God and you will find his rest.
Anxiety—concern caused by distrust in the Lord.

BJ trusted God. Everyone who knew him saw that. It seemed only fitting that the blog that gave updates on his physical condition would point others toward the same kind of trust: unrelenting, unceasing, and unashamed.

My family, my church, and many Peruvian brothers who worked with BJ are constantly praying for his health. We have to trust in and depend on our all-powerful Lord. I believe that God is preparing something incredible for all of our lives using BJ. God is the worker of miracles and he wants to perform miracles in BJ—in his family, his church, and in the whole world. Brothers, I encourage you to continue strongly in your faith: "Don't tell God how big the sickness is; tell the sickness how big your God is."

PASTOR TITO SEVILLA, BLOG POSTING
AUGUST 30, 2005 • TRANSLATED BY SAM BEER

This trust in a big and faithful God sustained the family through the surgery that transferred BJ to ECMO. It brought us through our own medical exams and round of antibiotics, a hospital response to the still-unidentified infection that had invaded BJ's body. It would carry us through the long hours and weeks ahead.

I want all of you to understand something. I am fully aware that my brother is FULLY in God's hands. We all agree that God has big plans for BJ. My terror in this whole situation is not that I don't trust what God is doing here. I have not forgotten my faith; I am leaning on it, and I know that God is not limited by this disease or his chances of survival. But the seriousness of it all is real, and the chances are real, and these are important facts in BJ's story and my family's overall understanding of and reaction to what is happening. We know that God will be glorified regardless of whether or not my brother dies. This is the hard part.

LAUREN, BLOG POSTING • AUGUST 20, 2005

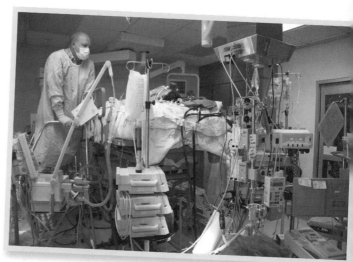

A jungle of medical equipment in his ECMO circuit

BJ's body continued its valiant fight, facing new challenges every few hours. Doctors continued their research, taking blood and tissue samples to test at the St. Vincent's lab and at the Centers for Disease Control (CDC) in Denver. We continued to connect with our young warrior, carefully mounting the steep metal staircases on each side of his bed (now elevated by a motorcycle lift to assist the gravity-driven ECMO pump) to stroke his hair or caress any small skin surface not entangled with tubing. And the body of Christ continued to follow BJ's example of trust in a sovereign God.

God answers prayer in all kinds of ways. . . . There are no coincidences. Everything in our lives, God orchestrates. So if one random event helps you get through a day, or if someone you prayed for gets better, that's not a coincidence or just something cool that happened to match up with your prayers, that is God working and answering your prayers.

IM CONVERSATION • JULY 26, 2005

Thank you for letting us be a part of praying for BJ. I remember my trip to The Gambia. I kept telling the team, "The crazier it gets, the bigger his story becomes!" . . . Rest assured that God is working a mighty act through BJ right now.

We love you and we will continue to pray with you and for you.

JOSHUA AND TIFFANY MCMILLIN, BLOG POSTING • SEPTEMBER 2, 2005

Almost as soon as www.prayforbj.com was online, the prayer warriors and bloggers received a dramatic boost—from an unexpected source. Rusty Kennedy was a longtime friend of MercyMe's lead singer, Bart Millard. He contacted him about praying for BJ, whom Bart had met—along with Dad—several years before.

Almost immediately, Bart began logging onto the blog, sometimes even posting anonymously. Soon he contacted Dad by phone. Bart's heartfelt response flowed from personal experience. Not long before, he had spent long days and nights at the hospital bedside of his own son, Sam, newly diagnosed with juvenile diabetes.

The conversation touched both men deeply. Somewhere in the midst of the tears and prayers, Bart asked what he could do to help. Dad explained that just before he entered the hospital, BJ had been studying John 17 and the unity of the body. Before machines and medication silenced his voice, he had asked his family to let the body of Christ know of his illness—so that more people could pray. That gave Bart an idea.

"If it's all right with you, I'll send out an email to our list. If we send it out, they'll pray. Just prepare for an onslaught!"

"Do it!" Dad told him. MercyMe posted a link to the blog on its website, and Bart wrote a letter introducing BJ's story, asking fans to join him in prayer.

I just had an email blast sent out to our MercyMe mailing list of around 200,000 to be praying for BJ, and I gave them the web address to stay on top of it. Hope that was ok.
I'm Bart Millard and I approve this email.

BART MILLARD, BLOG POSTING • AUGUST 23, 2005

I am a friend of Bart Millard's, and I just received word of your condition. My family and I are in prayer for you and your entire family. What the devil means for evil, God will use for the good. You may never know all the people you may touch for Christ even by having this website.

GINGER BEGGS, MICHIGAN, BLOG POSTING • AUGUST 23, 2005

Hi, I'm from Singapore (a tiny island country in South East Asia). I am on MercyMe's mailing list and got an Urgent Prayer Request from Bart. . . . BJ, fight a good fight! Don't let up!

BLOG POSTING • AUGUST 24, 2005

Throughout his hospital stay, BJ struggled to maintain an adequate blood oxygen level. ECMO helped, but his percentage numbers rose and fell. Doctors performed various procedures. Family, friends, and bloggers prayed. A blood drive was organized at Northside with donations credited to BJ, and prayer warriors offered to give in many other locations.

Before the end of August, the huge number of visitors to the blog site had us alternating between two main activities—checking the laptop to read the latest comments and standing at BJ's bedside to watch and pray. Already bloggers from more than forty states and several foreign countries had added their comments. Many of them posted multiple times.

Even the PICU medical staff showed deep interest in the blog. At home as well as at work, they regularly logged on for the latest updates. A faithful God was at work, drawing the caregivers, family, friends, and thousands of strangers back to www .prayforbj.com. In sickness and silence, BJ clung only to him.

God is in control of each situation, but sometimes he waits to answer or allows us to go through a hardship so that we can become stronger and rely more and more on him.

IM CONVERSATION • JULY 26, 2005

We checked the blog faithfully. . . . We'd be in the room, actually, and we would check it. We'd joke around. "Let's check and see how BJ's doing." A lot of it was to see how Brent and Deanna were doing. They would share their feelings, if they were up or down. It was kind of a little bit of insight for us.

DONNA GUIDER

Dear BJ, You are the best cousin. I like the way you help me and play with me. I can't wait to come and see you and when I grow up, I am going to move to Indiana and live next to Uncle Brent and Aunt Deanna's house so I can see you all the time. I love you.

JOSHUA DANZEISEN, BLOG POSTING • AUGUST 25, 2005

BJ and cousin Joshua

Just wanted to let you know that I passed on your blog site address to the folks at Focus on the Family. I got a reply: "Please be assured that we will also lift BJ up before the Lord's throne of grace this week when our staff gathers for devotions. We'll pray that God will bring peace to his mind and healing to his body in the days ahead."

CANDI, BLOG POSTING • AUGUST 25, 2005

I can remember when Deanna called, telling her, "In a few months, I can envision BJ going from one place to another, telling how Jesus miraculously cured him." We just never doubted that God would do it.

UNCLE DAN TUCKER

You are a popular young man. Almost 4400 people have made a visit to your site.

BLOG POSTING • AUGUST 29, 2005

As BJ lay in his hospital bed, his sisters were torn between school responsibilities and concern for their brother. Whitney's college semester had begun, and Lauren's would start soon.

167

Professors, papers, and tests. All seemed so insignificant compared to what BJ was going through. Still, our family and our many prayer partners continued to trust in God's unlimited power. A faithful God used these times of trial to move us toward the attitude BJ had written about in his journal in 2004:

Too often, we have the attitude where we need a sign before we believe that Christ will do a work, whereas our faith and his power should be sufficient. We should more often have the attitude of the woman in Luke 8:43–48 where our faith from him, in him, to him is enough.

Everything connected with BJ's journey seemed to start small, then explode—the illness, the blog, the blood drive, and even the "Pray for BJ" T-shirts that suddenly began to appear. A few Awe Star friends, some First Baptist Mooresville friends, and BJ's sisters (with their friend Rachel Gilliland) all designed and wore their shirts at about the same time. Everyone wanted to spread the word: pray for BJ.

The shirts that Lauren, Whitney, and Rachel made gave the www.prayforbj.com address, along with a verse that had appeared on the blog itself: "Therefore, since Christ suffered in his body, arm yourselves also with the same attitude, because he who has suffered in his body is done with sin. As a result, he does not live the rest of his earthly life for evil human desires, but rather for the will of God" (1 Peter 4:1–2 NIV).

Almost immediately, friends and family members were asking for shirts of their own. After some friendly prodding, Lauren arranged to have them printed. The chosen colors were pink (in honor of BJ's earlier choice of pink shirts for himself and his dad) and black (another of his favorites). When orders became unmanageable, Awe Star took over the shirt sales. The ministry covered all costs and offered to donate any proceeds to help with medical expenses. All told, over a thousand "Pray for BJ" shirts sold.

The calendar turned to September. The battle raged on. BJ's status advanced and retreated every few hours. Bleeding started. Bleeding stopped. Numbers rose. Numbers fell. Cannulas (medical tubing) were inserted. Cannulas were removed. Physicians anticipated the worst. God orchestrated the best, including a few scattered hours of alertness when BJ responded to us with a slight head turn or eye movement. Then the cycle began again. Through it all, we, and what had now become our blog family, continued to trust in the God of miracles.

Read Matthew 14:22 & 25–33. Try to imagine the disciples' fear and confusion at seeing Jesus walk on water. Many of us grew up with this story, but the disciples were completely dumbfounded. A man walking on water? How absurd! . . .

But even so, Peter focused his eyes on Christ and was able to do the supernatural with a natural body. However, when Peter started to doubt and look around, he lost sight of Christ; and so, he began to drown amidst the storm. This happens to many Christians, but in a less physical way. Perhaps this is what you are going through right now. People become Christians and focus on God, believing what he says and following his commands with faith.

But when the trials come, or in Peter's case, the storm, they begin to lose focus and look around, doubting. This is where we ALL fail. We start to doubt God and try to make it on our own, and like Peter, we will drown until Christ grabs us and pulls us back out.

"Milk" devotions • 2003

In early September, Satan tried another tactic. BJ's cultures began to come back positive for fungus. Earlier the ECMO tubing had been replaced in an effort to avoid this dangerous growth.

With the new evidence, physicians made the decision. The time had come to remove BJ from ECMO altogether.

The great cloud of prayer warriors again did battle on their knees. The process was scheduled then postponed, started then stopped. Throughout the uncertainty, bloggers continued to post, reassuring us that everyone connected with this procedure was covered in prayer.

In 2004 BJ came to our house in Tumbes, Peru. BJ was cool because he showed me how to do the sword fights. Every day I check about BJ and see how he is doing and I hope God will continue to heal him. Every day I pray for him in my class at Alliance Academy.

THOMAS LAMCA, MISSIONARY KID • QUITO, ECUADOR
BLOG POSTING • SEPTEMBER 5, 2005

Your steadfast faith is absolutely and completely inspiring. I am praying for your son and check the website daily. God bless you and your family during this tremendous trial you are enduring. Our God is an awesome God and miracles are right up his alley.

KIMBERLY PONCIN • PURCELLVILLE, VIRGINIA
BLOG POSTING • SEPTEMBER 15, 2005

When the removal from ECMO was finally complete, those who prayed for BJ had many reasons to rejoice. His oxygen levels had improved dramatically. His lung X-rays looked amazingly clear. He was breathing once again with only the aid of the oscillating ventilator. Even the removal of two liters of blood (clotted within his chest cavity) and the discovery of an unidentified mass in his left lung had not halted the procedure. Most miraculous of all, the looming danger of clots in the cannulas had been completely avoided. Our family and our many prayer supporters knew the source of BJ's amazing strength. It was the same as our own.

I have been praying for you every day, many times two, three, or more times. My heart really does break for you right now, and I pray that you are finding rest in the shadow of God's wings. I find that whenever I am broken or in a valley, Psalm 91 is always uplifting. Just try to remember that God is our strength, and that he loves us and gives us rest though we are constantly waging war.

EMAIL CORRESPONDENCE • NOVEMBER 20, 2004

He beat the records so many times! When they were trying to bring him off ECMO, they had to take him off the blood thinners. They were desperately concerned about this, because it would eventually clot off the pump. This was one of those miraculous things that happened. In the end, the time it took to actually clot off was so much longer than had ever happened before. God just kept it going!

Dad

I could probably count a dozen different times that the medical staff believed: "I don't think he's gonna make it through this." The Higgins family would post the request, and he would come through just fine. There were days he was doing really bad, and then he would take an upswing. There were little surprises all along the way that made you think, *Wow, was that really just about all the people praying?*

DONNA GUIDER

Section Six

The Legacy

Be still, and know that I am God; I
will be exalted among the nations,
I will be exalted in the earth!

PSALM 46:10

seventeen

Haste the Day

1 Peter 1:6b–7: Suffering is a mercy from God because it allows us to make much of Christ, and it makes much of Christ, who is the sole thing that satisfies. Our trials bring glory to God (so take joy in them). . . . John 17:22: God gave Christ glory, who gave us glory. As we give God glory, he glorifies us in him. Suffering brings God glory, and therefore brings us glory. Also, to glorify God, or to receive glory, we must go through suffering.

> *God glorifies us when we suffer.*
> *To have glory, you must suffer.*
> *To bring God glory, you will suffer.*
> *To suffer brings God glory.*

BJ Higgins
Peru Journal • July 20, 2005

Suffer for his glory.

More than forty states. Over fifty countries. Six of the seven continents. Prayforbj.com received hundreds of hits every day

and postings from bloggers in every one of these places. Countless others read and prayed without writing a word. With so
many prayers being lifted on all sides, why did BJ continue to
struggle?

As usual, he already knew the answer. The relentless attacks
on his battle-weary body allowed him, once again, to live what
he believed. His recent Bible studies had uncovered an important
truth: *God uses suffering to reveal his glory.* And BJ, his body swollen
by the barrage of medications and scarred by the assaults of the
unknown infection, was definitely suffering. The words he had
written in 2002 rang true: "No action is greater than its motive.
The only correct motive is to bring glory to God."

The CDC had not yet returned results on the exact source of
his illness. Eventually, however, doctors decided that the danger
of the infection had passed. They released BJ from the restric-
tions of isolation.

After the weeks of dramatic ups and downs, our family trea-
sured the rare moments of quiet, times when we could momen-
tarily relax. Even on those easier days, however, serious medical
concerns remained. BJ's kidneys had not yet functioned without
assistance. His lungs developed air pockets that hindered their
work. Bruises and other wounds (indicating tissue breakdown)
appeared on his skin. As one of the charge nurses told us early
on, "This is a book, and it happens in chapters. We have many
more chapters to go."

Another chapter began to unfold with the sudden news, late in
September, that BJ's white cell count had spiked. This signaled a
new or increasing infection—but where? Doctors examined and
consulted. We prayed and called our prayer warriors to renewed
activity. The days of battle rested solidly on the glory of God.

*For when you have joy in God's awesomeness, thus you are
in praise, you will feel compelled to share it and spread it.*

Praise of God alone will make you realize that you are small, insignificant, and useless. Then you will find yourself glorifying God, and not yourself, for you are nothing, and God is everything; and for our nothing, God sacrificed everything, so that we may have everything.

PERSONAL JOURNAL • CA. 2003

As the Knightmare in Awe Star's "Freedom" drama, BJ had perfectly portrayed Satan's evil dance. He leaped high in the air. He spun. He lunged. He drew back. He twirled his swords. He marched. He slashed. The one who so passionately pursued God's glory was able to capture the dark, desperate acts of the one who seeks only to lie, steal, and destroy.

Swordfight between BJ as Satan and David as Christ

In room 2001 of St. Vincent's Hospital, the dance played out once more. This time, however, the drama was all too real. In Peru the Enemy's tactics proved ineffective. In the hospital, he pulled out even more of his arsenal, intensifying the conflict with his small but persistent foe. Policemen with uzis had not stopped either his witness or God's glory. Would the raging illness?

> BJ, I want to express my pain for you as you're going through this. As Paul said, "When one part of the body suffers, they all suffer." But I also want to encourage you by saying that the Enemy is scared of you! You're going through this spiritual

warfare because they are trying to stop you at all costs; they know you will do great things for the Kingdom of God; and they're TERRIFIED! . . . Praying for you, brother.

PJ Accetturo, student missionary • Panama 2005
blog posting • August 30, 2005

BJ's sword had long been unsheathed. Now he battled for his life as never before. His blood pressure and oxygen saturation (SAT) scores plummeted. Surgeons rushed to drain fluid from his lungs. They worked to treat festering wounds on his hip and back. Relentlessly, inexhaustibly, the Enemy pressed in. The visible battle seemed endless, and the invisible realm was engaged in an even greater struggle. Throughout the hours of suffering, God's glory prevailed, and victory was assured.

Every thirty minutes the oven timer goes off and we go to our knees again for BJ. . . . Wow!! Look at the body of Christ joining you in prayer. . . . He continually amazes us!! To God be the Glory!!

blog posting • September 23, 2005

My little brother is amazing. He is laying down his life right now. He is eager to suffer for his Father's glory. He GETS it. And I am challenged on a whole new level to understand that ALL is for God's glory.

Lauren • blog posting • September 2, 2005

October 1—BJ's sixteenth birthday—drew closer. His battle continued. Even as the prognosis darkened, our family and the blog family held on to hope, pressing on in our pursuit of God's glory.

Also, as the apostles are constantly reminding us in their letters, we have a hope and a certainty for the future that no

178

one else has. *We know that at the end of all things, Christ will gather us together and reveal his glory to the world on the day of judgment. Instead of receiving the judgment and condemnation that we deserve, we will be able to take part in the GLORY of Christ.*

So then, let us with his glory and our hope in mind, throw down our lives and pick up his—that is, pick up our cross, take our life of suffering for him and his glory. Let us die daily for Christ so that we can follow him and better obey his call: that we reach the dying people of this world and tell them of Jesus Christ, the saving One.

Whew. So that's what God is teaching me.

WWW.XANGA.COM/DEADSILENCE7 • AUGUST 2, 2005

> We do not know the timing or the outcome, but we continue to push on. We pray . . . that Jesus' name be glorified in these hours.
>
> Dad
> blog posting • September 26, 2005

I can't sleep; I can't get BJ off my mind. I will stay awake and continue to pray. God bless you . . . and comfort BJ.

BLOG POSTING • SEPTEMBER 26, 2005

God, give each one, Deanna, Brent, Whitney, and Lauren, what they need to go through these hours. They still long to glorify you no matter what. Strengthen them, comfort them, let each one feel your very presence in a new way, in a physical way, that would grant them peace and restoration.

DEBBIE LINDER • BLOG POSTING • SEPTEMBER 26, 2005

BJ had unsheathed his sword. He had picked up his life of suffering. Early in the morning of September 26, he laid it all down at last, entering into glory with his God.

179

Family prayer circle on BJ's 16th birthday

I remember standing there watching the screen, thinking, "I'm watching him die. His vitals are going down." As soon as he flatlined, the medical team turned everything off and got all the equipment out of the room. They were so great, letting us get close to him that one last time.

There were a bunch of nurses and other medical people standing there. Some had come in who weren't working but had been with us all the way through. I didn't know what to do . . . one of the nurses came over and hugged me, and I just let her . . . I remember the nurses' faces as they walked in.

All this has definitely had an impact on my plans for my career. I still don't know what kind of nurse I want to be. I'm thinking more now about doing Pediatric ICU just because I've been there. The biggest thing is that I know what it's like to spend that kind of time in the hospital with someone who's sick, and I know how much the nurses meant to our family. Part of me wants to be that [kind of caregiver] to a family, to help a family get through that.

———

WHITNEY

That night, Mom told me to go back to school, that they would call me if anything changed. I was doing laundry and talking to a friend when my phone rang. It was Whitney. She said, "We think you should come back."

In that one moment, so many thoughts went through my head. BJ had had a bad weekend. Whitney was calling because Mom and Dad couldn't. I couldn't quite grasp what that meant.

My three roommates grabbed their pillows, and we took off for the hospital. In the car, I told them stories about BJ while they prayed.

The whole trip seemed surreal. My mind kept flashing back and forth between our conversation and his hospital room. I felt like I could almost see the bad things happening in BJ's room. I knew it wasn't good. I knew he was getting worse.

LAUREN

I never felt as though God promised me that BJ would be healed, but I did not know his illness was unto death. I was always hopeful, to the very last day. When I look back on all the traumatic times, I realize I was never really alarmed. That's unexplainable and something that only happens with prayer support. God gave us a special kind of peace.

Mom

When BJ passed, I stopped. I watched for a moment to see if something was going to happen. I had no doubt that God could raise him up if he chose to do so. I was resting my hands on either side of the IV posts. I went to stand up, and immediately felt someone lift me up. I turned to see who it was, to offer my thanks. I turned from side to side. There was no one there.

Dad

As untold numbers wept and prayed, more than six hundred responded—some almost immediately—to Dad's message, posted within thirty minutes of his son's death: "Just before 3 this morning, my precious BJ went home to be with all of our precious Jesus. 'Well done, thou good and faithful servant.' My God is a God of compassion . . . 'it is finished.'"

In BJ's death, as in his life, God's glory blazed.

All of us who were praying and watching with you are now grieving with you as well. . . . May our Lord hold you close to his heart and continue to sustain you . . . and through our tears, may he be praised.

Angie • blog posting • September 26, 2005

There are no words that will ease your pain right now, but I wanted to let you know how much you all and BJ have affected every life you touched at St. Vincent's. No matter what time of day we saw you, you had a smile. You asked about others even during the most difficult days for BJ. You showed us all what true love and compassion really is. While we were not able to save BJ, I know that God placed him in our unit, in our city for a reason. He especially changed my life.

While I cry along with you and my heart breaks for your loss, I rejoice knowing that BJ is probably talking God's ear off, and he's not getting the "short version." I can't wait to see him again someday!! All our love from St. V's.

blog posting • September 26, 2005

I praise our Father. . . . Through the tears I truly know that God has been and will be more glorified in this. . . . Father, ignite in us all the fire to truly live for you, focusing on your glory and that alone. Send us out with the story of BJ and his faithfulness to you. May you continue to be glorified!

Tara Case, student missionary • Peru 2005
blog posting • September 26, 2005

BJ would never have considered death his true enemy. He "got it" about that as well, writing in his 2003 autobiography:

My brightest moment, which will be beyond anything that anyone in this world can imagine, and also that will last forever, is spending eternity in heaven with my Lord.

Over the six-week vigil, friends and family asked. Even those who never asked wondered: *What is wrong with BJ?*

The answer remains shrouded in confusion—another of the Enemy's deceptive tactics. The dual round of antibiotics, prescribed early on, masked the test results. Every symptom pointed to one disease. CDC specialists sought hard evidence. Only one culture came back positive. A definitive diagnosis required two. However, every intensivist who examined him, and every Peruvian doctor who studied the reports, believed that BJ had contracted bubonic plague.

BJ himself would not want the focus of attention to be on his illness and death. Instead, he would point our attention to the God he served—the God who has all authority over every circumstance and situation. As he began to experience his first symptoms, BJ never once expressed surprise. He was already suffering for the glory of God—and he knew that regardless of the outcome, he could continue to trust his loving heavenly Father. In July, in one of his last IM conversations with his good friend Jack Meils, BJ wrote, "Well, I'll see you sometime, or else in heaven."

In the midst of our grief, we were surprised when we began receiving hints of something our young missionary had wisely avoided telling us. During his second mission trip, God had called him to lay down his life for the cause of Christ—to become a martyr. BJ had spoken about this calling with only a select few—first in Peru, then in Indianapolis.

As we began to hear more about our son's call to martyrdom, we were more and more amazed. Only a merciful God could have kept BJ's Awe Star teammates, friends, and family members healthy despite their close contact with BJ. Only a sovereign God could have orchestrated events so that the body of Christ united so wonderfully during his six weeks of hospitalization. And only a powerful God would continue to speak through BJ's death— even more clearly and effectively than through his life.

Philippians: Living is all for Christ and entails many trials and persecution, and is better for those around you, but dying and going to be with the Lord is better for yourself. We need to live with courage and character worthy of citizens of heaven, fight boldly in this spiritual war we are immersed in, and take our suffering boldly, for it is a pleasure to suffer for Christ.

PERU JOURNAL • JULY 4, 2004

BJ had heard another missionary share at ASU about being called to give his life for Christ. We had a conversation on the bus going to Cajamarca when he said, "I feel like God is calling me one day to give my life for Christ—but I'm still praying about it." He was very humble about his call to become a martyr.

BARBARA ANN SHEELY • PERU 2005

He and I talked a lot about the calling to be a martyr. I could tell that God was putting it on his heart. He never said it aloud to me, but it was always on his mind: "If I die, this is how I want to go."

LOGAN SHIELDS • PERU 2005

At Jump Start, BJ told us that this passion wouldn't be unnoticed by Satan, that he was going to be a martyr somehow. Satan wasn't going to let things happen that easily. BJ was definitely expecting to be a martyr, or at least attacked.

ERIC DAVID

BJ shared with some friends at Jump Start that he felt called to be a martyr. He said he felt like Satan was going to attack him physically. None of us really realized it would happen so soon.

Jack Meils

I remember him saying at Jump Start, "In a month I could be unconscious in the hospital. In two months, I could be dead." He told us, "I don't know how much time I have, but I know that I'm going to spend it telling about the love of God and the grace of God."

Brittany DiSalvo

We were talking during the Jump Start weekend about what the Lord had done in us over the summer. He was just very passionate, telling me about the missionary movement that he believed God would usher in. There was something very strange about the atmosphere. God was the most real thing in that room, the most real thing around that experience. It was as though BJ had already died, and God was the only One talking. BJ was gone.

We continued walking and talking. We were both being excited about whatever God was doing in our lives. At that point, he took me over to the side and said something like, "Don't tell anybody this, but I believe that God's going to make me a martyr."

Wes Cate

eighteen

Memorial Calling

¡Aquí Estoy!
(Here Am I!)

Tonight was awesome . . . as David came "as an empty man" and taught compellingly about our true identity in Christ. In the realest form of reality, I am not BJ Higgins, son of Brent, the sinner; for he is dead. I am the righteous prince, BJ Christ, son of the King of Kings.

BJ HIGGINS
PERU JOURNAL • JUNE 24, 2004

Find your identity in Christ.

It had ended.

It had only begun.

The family—Dad, Mom, Lauren, and Whitney—stumbled back home and into what we began to call the "new normal"—the one where nothing seemed normal at all. The first painful days after BJ's death overflowed with phone calls, conversations, decisions, and details. Still numb with grief, we floated in an emotional and spiritual haze. Just as they had during the weeks of hospitalization, hundreds of postings from our family of bloggers provided welcome, comforting contact.

> I shared my story of BJ tonight at Bible study. I told them how BJ has influenced my walk with Christ more than any other event in my life (next to the day I handed my life over to him). Thank you to God for allowing us a look into the life of a wonderful Christian, BJ, who is now by his side, smiling.
>
> BLOG POSTING • SEPTEMBER 27, 2005

> Thank you so very much for taking time to let us, the body of Christ, know some of the details. Like so many others have said, checking this site has become a part of my daily routine. I remember in one of my first posts, I said that I could see BJ as a walking testimony to the Lord's faithfulness and love. I firmly believe that this is still true. BJ is now walking the streets of gold with our precious Savior, and there in heaven he is still touching and changing lives for the King and his kingdom.
>
> LINDA RONNE • BLOG POSTING • SEPTEMBER 27, 2005

For our family the most important, immediate decision was how to celebrate BJ's life. BJ's friend Jack told us that BJ had expressed the desire that when he died, he didn't want tears; he wanted a party—a celebration—something spectacular that would give all the glory to God. Making no promises about the tears, we set about to plan the kind of memorial that would allow us to remember our BJ. It would focus, above all, on honoring his God.

Open for me the gates where the righteous enter and I will go and thank the Lord." That blows my mind—that we are righteous enough in Christ that we can say, "Open up the gates to where the Lord dwells and only the righteous can enter and I will go in and speak with the Lord."

PERU JOURNAL • JULY 2, 2004

Numerous Indiana bloggers, friends from all three churches, and the Higgins-Tucker extended family all planned to attend the memorial celebration. Our Awe Star family made every effort to come as well. On the afternoon and evening of Thursday, September 29, our family would host a memorial calling (visitation) at Northside Baptist. The following afternoon at four, Pastors Larry Floyd and Rusty Kennedy, Dr. Walker Moore, and others would share at the memorial celebration, also at Northside. The entire Awe Star staff planned to fly in on Wednesday. The next evening two vans would leave from Tulsa for Indiana. These vans would transport the

Our family at BJ's memorial celebration

many student missionaries—including many of our son's Peru teammates—who wanted to attend the memorial celebration.

People were coming from all directions to honor God's servant and to give God glory for what he had done. The autopsy performed that week revealed even more evidence of God's work. It went beyond his immediate cause of death to describe the terrible damage caused by the Enemy's wounds. The pathologist who wrote up the report added a question that his data alone could not answer: "How did this young man last as long as he did?"

> His tissues and organs were so badly damaged from the initial infection that despite the heroic efforts and measures of the St. Vincent's staff, he had no chance of survival. . . . We know that our Lord Jesus Christ and the "great cloud of witnesses" sustained his life through intercessory prayer . . . so that others could know the Savior. We are humbled and grateful that the Lord would choose to use our BJ in such a way.
>
> Dad
> blog posting • September 27, 2005

Knowing the Word. Having a heartbeat of obedience. Suiting up in the armor. Unsheathing his sword. All helped answer the doctor's question about BJ's endurance. Another factor, like so many of the others, made itself evident in his written words—already a significant part of our young warrior's legacy.

As we began to explore his writing, one thing seemed overwhelmingly clear. The BJ who witnessed to his teacher and classmates through a school composition was the same BJ who shared the gospel in Peru or IMed a friend who wanted to meet Jesus. The BJ who shared his spiritual struggles in his journal was the same BJ who posted about them on his Xanga weblog. The BJ who served his Peru teammates by washing dishes also served his First Baptist, Mooresville, friends by clearing the tables during their Kentucky mission trip.

> I just want to take a few moments and tell everyone about the BJ that I know. I know BJ as a guy that just wants to see the nations come to know [Christ] as Lord and Savior. BJ is one that is not afraid to talk to anyone and weeps when people say no to knowing [Christ]. He is a guy that when we get up in the

morning will make you laugh and will always have something very deep that God has taught him. He is not afraid of telling people what he has learned and is always looking for someone to tell them about what God is doing in his life. He is a joy to be around. Even when he is sick, most of the time you would never know, since he won't tell you unless you make him say how he is feeling. He is the guy that makes everyone feel good about himself, and he is the one that a lot of people look towards for encouragement. He is helpful when he knows he can help and will do anything you ask him to do. He is just a great man of God to be around and learn from.

DAVID POST • BLOG POSTING • AUGUST 28, 2005

BJ was radically consistent because he knew exactly who he was. Even at a young age, he was a man—a man who understood his identity in Christ. As early as 2002, he had recorded a truth that many older Christians fail to grasp: "What is true of Christ is true of us."

BJ had not come to this understanding on his own. It had been emphasized and reemphasized by his youth pastor, Rusty Kennedy, and then reinforced through the Awe Star teachings of Walker Moore and David Post.

About five years ago, I really came to understand my own personal identity—who I was in Jesus. The years before that, it was all about my youth ministry and about the church— how good it could be. All of that became less important than understanding who I was as a saint, a believer, one who was redeemed and justified and glorified in Christ.

After that became real to me, for the last three years in student ministry, that's all I taught. I think BJ understood. On the field, and when he returned home, that was the battle he had with Satan: he was being deceived about who he was. When he came home and said he was going to be a man, he

190

understood the battle he was in—that explains his obsession with the sword.

Satan wants to deceive us as a church, to tell us we are lowly sinners saved by grace. BJ "got it" about his identity: I'm absolutely worthy, I'm absolutely holy, I'm justified, I'm a holy nation, a royal priesthood—not because of anything I did, but because of what Christ has done in me.

Pastor Rusty Kennedy

Then I started remembering (or God started reminding) what God is teaching me about who I am. This is what I know so far, from this trip: I am a righteous prince, a son of God, with God's inheritance and authority and power through the Holy Spirit living in me. I have a thirst for knowledge and for God and a heart for service. The song "Adopted by the King" has always stuck out to me, especially the line "and he changed my name."

God has a new name for me, but my pride has been blinding me to who I am in Christ because it took over who I was. So now, as God is slowly lifting . . . the scales from my eyes, I am starting to discover who I am in Christ—that is, who I am.

Personal Journal • July 8, 2004

Once BJ had established his true identity in Christ and secured it during his days on the mission field, he was ready. He could do what he always did: live out what he believed and immediately begin to teach others. In the fall of 2004, when he wrote the passionate cry to "raise a revolution," he also sent an email to his Awe Star teammates describing lessons he learned from John Eldredge's book *Wild at Heart* (Thomas Nelson, 2001).

Eldredge points out something I had been struggling with without even knowing it. He says that rather than hiding your strength (passion, wisdom, God-given knowledge, maturity, and authority) because the world has no room for it and people can't

*handle it, let it loose, and let them deal with it and stare on in
wonder at the incredible things that God has done and is doing.
Now, I am praying that God would give me the courage to reveal
my strength to those around me, that I might show them who I
am now that God is in me and has transformed me. . . .*

*Here I come: a warrior, a prince, son of God, and I am righteous
and armed with God's suit of armor, and backed by the power and
authority of Jesus Christ himself, for he lives in me.*

We wanted to tell the world about God's work in and through
BJ's life. We would start with those attending the memorial
calling and celebration. Friends helped assemble photo collages
and other displays that captured BJ as a baby; as a young child;
and especially as a man, a righteous prince and warrior for Jesus
Christ. At both the calling and celebration, his sword would take
a prominent place. The Bible verses he was memorizing when
he left for Peru that summer—including the ones that introduce
each section of this book—formed another key display.

Before the three o'clock starting hour on the day of the memorial calling, the crowd began to gather. We stood at the front
of Northside's expansive sanctuary as long lines of visitors began
to file in.

Big John, the family's protector and advisor, and a team of
friends worked tirelessly to make the time less grueling for us.
They made sure that we took occasional breaks, and they kept
the lines moving as smoothly as possible. For example, when
the medical team from St. Vincent's arrived, Big John made
sure they immediately moved to the front, encouraged Dad to
introduce them, and initiated a round of applause from the
entire assembly.

One of the physicians wanted us all to go as a group. The way
that they had it set up, you went through the foyer in the

192

church. The Higgins family's response to us when we walked in was like when you go home to your family—you're being welcomed back again, you're with family again.

Diana Massmalmhoff, RN • St. Vincent's Hospital

At one point when we were up front, they wanted a photo with all of us. We got into place for a group photo, and I believe everybody stood up and started clapping. You could almost see people talking: "That's the doctor, those are the nurses." You would expect a standing ovation if we *saved* somebody's life—it was extremely humbling.

Donna Guider

All told, more than a thousand people moved through the lines that afternoon and evening. Dad had urged bloggers to identify themselves, and many of them did, via nametags given to them at the door. In many ways, the memorial calling mirrored the blog experience in its tears, prayer, celebration, and sense of awe. BJ would have been embarrassed by all the attention. No doubt, he would also have been amazed by the overriding sense of unity and love.

When we asked Walker Moore to speak the next day, we gave him an apt description of what we believed should take place: "a BJ service." Walker knew that this meant a service reflecting BJ's dual passions: knowing the Savior and taking the message to every nation. The celebration should provide opportunity for people to surrender to both.

The average desires of a normal teenager? Yes and no. BJ's life

BJ in Peru

193

represented a "new normal"—not because he was perfect, but because of his obedient service to an all-powerful God. This young man found his identity not in a list of accomplishments, not in his admiring peers, not even in his beloved family, but in Christ alone.

John James Peter Timothy Isaiah David Christ, a slave of Jesus Christ, a righteous prince and holy son of God. A passionate saint and a courageous warrior in the army of the Lord Almighty, having all of the power and authority of Jesus Christ because he lives in him. Heir of heaven, called to disciple and serve the peoples of the earth with God-given gifts of teaching, knowledge, and serving. A man of God and leader among his friends. Having the Holy Spirit dwelling in, covering, and working through him. Endowed with passion and intensity, having the powerful characteristic of leadership. Called into manhood and realized his call to God's ministry as well as fervently seeking to carry out his calling and grow spiritually at a young age. Called to become humble and pure in heart. Called to a partnership in ministry, with his brother, aimed mainly to his own nation, but also periodically to travel to other areas of the world, spreading the Good News. Has a God-given passion and talent for music. Ambitious and seeking to be a vessel through which God accomplishes great things. Can be compared to the circulatory system in the body of Christ, a lion, eagle, horse, or wolf in character. Jesus Christ is a light in the dark world through him. Given name of Brent Allen Higgins, Jr., or BJ.

To God be the Glory.
(signed) James Timothy Christ
Brent Higgins, Jr.
2005

nineteen

Memorial Celebration

¡Envíame me!
(Send me!)

And so now I challenge you, if you are not involved in missions or supporting missions to do so, for each of us has a different task to do in the body of Christ, as it says in Romans 12, but we are all to work together for the glory of God. And I also challenge and encourage you to continue to grow in Christ, daily reading his Word, praying, worshiping, and fellowshiping. Do not be satisfied with staying the same person and doing the same mundane routine each day, but change, grow closer to God and move deeper than just ankle-deep in him every day you live, for it may very well be your last.

BJ Higgins

WWW.XANGA.COM/DEADSILENCE7 • OCTOBER 11, 2004

Take my place.

The memorial calling and its constant flow of visitors served as a small glimpse of God's plans for the celebration to take place the following day. Throughout much of his life, BJ was known for speaking beyond the moment. The further he went in his relationship with Christ, the more obvious this quality became.

Friends and family knew that, even in the most intimate conversations, he had a serious message to share—a message that went beyond the moment and beyond his immediate audience. As his close friend Jack Meils says, "You always knew that BJ was speaking to the masses." All those who knew him—in life or only through the blog—knew that even death could not silence his voice. The more he grew in the Lord, the more passionate that voice had been in challenging friends and family to heed God's call. Not only did BJ accept God's call to travel to Peru and North Africa, but he also wanted others to join him in taking the gospel to the people of the world.

And now, I want to challenge you to take part as well in the Great Commission, and go to the nations (which include America as well), and somehow get involved in missions, whether by financial support or training or going to a foreign country yourself, because God called us to share his name, and when we are obedient, he does great things.

PERU JOURNAL • JULY 21, 2004

I love you BJ! I'm really gonna miss you . . . but I'm not going to let this make me angry at God. I'm just going to use this to make me fight harder to get the Lord's work done . . . 'cause it's what you'd want me to do.

HEATHER SCHAPER • PERU 2005
BLOG POSTING • SEPTEMBER 26, 2005

I was made aware of this website back in August from a coworker. I have checked it daily since. . . . I, myself, have just begun reading my Bible and attending church. I can honestly say that your son has inspired me to know more and to begin a relationship with God. BJ really "got it." The word has spread throughout our country about BJ and he will continue to be an inspiration to all of us.

CHRISTY K • INDIANAPOLIS
BLOG POSTING • SEPTEMBER 26, 2005

Our hearts are broken for your family. You are continually in our thoughts and prayers. BJ has impacted my life forever. I will keep his journal entries with me in a collection of life-changing writings I have accumulated over many years. I want you to know that God has used your son to refocus me in his kingdom work.

LYNNE HUTTO ALBANESE • GRAY, GEORGIA
BLOG POSTING • SEPTEMBER 26, 2005

BJ never stopped speaking to the masses. The day of the memorial celebration, his friends, Awe Star teammates, pastors, and other mentors would give resounding voice to a message that Satan had desperately tried to silence: *Take my place.* The passionate plea emailed to his Awe Star teammates after their 2004 trip now reached many other ears.

So here is my prayer and battle cry: Let a work even greater than what we saw in Peru be done here in the States! We saw hundreds come to him in five weeks, so how much more can he do with eleven months, this time with seventeen different ministry teams, not just four or five?! . . .

Just as so many people in Tumbes, Piura, and Trujillo hit their knees and finally realized God's love for them and so gave glory to him, now as we have been dispersed . . . may people [everywhere] hit their knees in worship of the one, true, and living God!! Amen.

AUGUST 8, 2004

BJ had requested a party with a purpose: the glory of God. The memorial celebration at Northside Baptist one day before his sixteenth birthday would have surpassed his wildest dreams.

Next to his Savior, BJ loved his family. Every one of his remaining grandparents, aunts, uncles, and first cousins—along with other extended family members—came to his party. Driving and flying from as far away as California, Texas, North Carolina, and Virginia, they came to support their loved ones and honor God's work in BJ's life.

BJ loved worship music. His party had plenty—from his own First Baptist Mooresville praise team and from worship leaders/ artists Billy and Cindy Foote, who flew in for the celebration from their Texas home.

BJ loved Peru. Pastor Tito Sevilla and missionary Frank Lamca both made the long trek from South America to pay tribute to (as Tito later put it) "a great small servant of God." Both counted the opportunity worthy of the sacrifice.

BJ loved his friends. Crowds of his brothers and sisters in Christ (from Awe Star, Northside, Crosswinds, Mooresville, and www.prayforbj.com) filled the sanctuary. Several of them spoke words of love and encouragement from the platform. One of them even tap-danced there to the glory of God—just the way BJ had encouraged her to do.

I know through the life of BJ that not even death can separate us from the Lord. The name of the Lord will continue to be preached. BJ is with the Lord, but those people that came to know the Lord because BJ preached to them will continue to win souls. I think that for those of us who knew BJ, the best way to remember him is to continue the work that he began.

PASTOR TITO SEVILLA

I knew God was calling me to a ministry with the performing arts. It was encouraging to me that BJ would talk about tap-dancing as ministry; he really thought that was me.

KELSEY BARNETT, FAMILY FRIEND

We're here today at this memorial celebration because BJ was obedient. He realized that the King is coming back. There's not a lot of time left.

BILLY J. FOOTE, MUSICIAN AND WORSHIP LEADER

Finally, BJ loved to challenge others. His own words, the music, the testimonies of his friends, and the powerful preaching allowed him to—as Walker Moore said about his ministry in Peru—"call forth salvation out of the multitudes" once again.

Read Matthew 7:21–23. Many people try to be "good people," and think that that is enough to get them to heaven. However, it says right here that more is required. A personal relationship with Jesus is absolutely necessary to get to heaven. As Jesus said in John 14:6 (NLT), "I am the way, the truth, and the life. No one can come to the Father except through me."

"MILK" DEVOTIONS • 2003

Just as BJ had done so boldly and so often in Peru, Dr. Moore clearly set forth the gospel. He invited those who received Jesus to indicate their decision by raising their hands. Eight individuals did so. Next, he launched into what he considered an imperative but frightening part of his message. Describing the global mission fields where he had taken thousands of students through the years, he challenged everyone present: "Who will take BJ's place?"

I knew the message about answering the call to take the gospel to the nations was for more than just the Higgins family—that

199

it was for this generation. I asked the Lord to help me give hope to the family but also to have a message that would stand on its own.

It was very risky—what if no one came forward to take his place? How would the Higgins family feel?

WALKER MOORE

Don't be the reason your kids aren't in God's will! Don't you be the roadblock. That's the very opposite of what BJ stood for. You cannot be the reason your kids don't go.

Mom

If God has called you or your child to the mission field, you are accountable to him for your decision. You do not have our permission to use BJ as your excuse.

Dad

At the service, when Walker asked who would take BJ's place, I immediately felt a strong urging to stand and go in place of my little brother. Later the four of us decided that we wanted to go as a family to North Africa because of the calling he had felt to serve there. We all felt sure that we were to go.

WHITNEY

It frustrates me that some parents are so overprotective of their children that they won't ever let them go on a mission trip. The

parents don't respect the maturity of their kids. The only reason not to let a child go is if you know it's not God's will. When you don't let them go out of fear, it's wrong.

Seeing my parents still do it [allow their children to serve in international missions, as Lauren and Whitney both did within the year following BJ's death] after such a tragedy is amazing. Serving God is the only response that makes sense, and

BJ's sisters holding an unsheathed sword the first Christmas after his death missions is such an opportunity for growth. If you don't let your kids go, you may be failing to let them do God's will.

LAUREN

Walker's challenge—BJ's challenge—evoked an immediate, overwhelming response. The sanctuary air filled with the haunting strains of "Rescue the Perishing." The front of the church also filled—with students answering the call.

First to rise and move forward was BJ's cousin Joshua, age six. He understood the task that God laid on his heart. He and ninety-six others were ready. They stepped forward. They crossed the line. Each one was surrendering time, finances, and most important, *life* to take BJ's place.

Joshua holding an unsheathed sword symbolizing BJ's life

I would love to tell you more stories of the things that God did [in Peru] sometime. . . . But most importantly, God challenged me and my team to lay down our lives for him and to live the LIFESTYLE of a missionary.

It's so easy, in the USA, to get comfortable with where we are and to get comfortable, even, with our small ministry or lack thereof, but God did not call us to a life of comfort, but to a life of suffering for him, which brings us JOY and GLORY through Jesus Christ. Christ doesn't just call us to live for him on Sundays and Wednesdays, or on camps and mission trips, or during Bible studies and SV or FCA meetings, but EVERY DAY, every moment of our lives. *God taught me that even my "home" town is a mission field (since we are aliens in this world, and it is not our home).*

It's time that we as Christians stop being lazy and just talking the talk, and get our hands and feet dirty actually following him and serving him diligently every day of our lives. We need to take his message to the people of every nation—including ours (for we all know how much our nation needs Christ). He went through the blood; the least we can do is go through the mud.

WWW.XANGA.COM/DEADSILENCE7 • JULY 25, 2005

What Walker said put an exclamation point on anything that had been stirred up in Joshua's heart before. He meant it. He understood it. He talks about it still.

AUNT LYNAE

The celebration service was amazing on Friday, and that people accepted Christ during it made it even better. The speaker who gave the message was very right in saying that BJ was a leader to the students. During Jump Start, BJ told me the same exact story of how he became a man, and from that point on, I always looked at him differently....The whole ordeal with BJ has really made me want to go on missions around the world.

MARISSA BALOG • BLOG POSTING • OCTOBER 2, 2005

twenty

I Would Die for You

Also, in another passage . . . it says, "Greater love has no man than this, that he lay down his life for his friends." This passage has a double meaning. One, that Christ is the ultimate example of love (being that he is God and God is love), and two, that the GREATEST love is to sacrifice yourself for your friends. [When I say love is a verb], this is the action I'm talking about. Not necessarily to literally get killed to save someone, but to lay your life down: to become selfless and act for others instead of yourself, or to devote your life.

BJ HIGGINS
FROM A 2004 LETTER

You never know why you're alive until you know what you would die for.

Students who introduce Awe Star's "Freedom" drama to a watching crowd describe it as containing two stories. "The first one, you can see with your eyes. It's about a good prince, a gentle ruler, the people of the land, and an evil dragon. The second story is harder to see. You can see it only with your heart. As you watch our drama, look for the second story."

Multiple facets come together to form the story of BJ Higgins: a son, leaning on his parents to show his love—and never really knowing how to give them the "short version" of anything. A brother, arguing vehemently that "Love is a verb." A student, intentionally designing school papers and presentations as avenues for sharing Christ. A man, coming forward in instant obedience to lay his adolescence at the altar. A black-masked Knightmare, portraying Satan with dramatic leaps and sinister slashes. A missionary adventurer, daring to share the gospel even with those who seemed least likely to respond. A critically ill patient, selflessly expressing concern for his nurse and his family between gulps of oxygen. A warrior, unsheathing his sword for battle. A martyr, willing to suffer and die for the glory of God.

BJ's story grew larger—and faster—than anyone anticipated. The thousands of blog postings and prayers from locations all over the world demonstrated that. So did the large number of people who came to the memorial calling and celebration, and the amazing response from those who stood ready to take BJ's place. In his death, as in his life, BJ spoke to the masses.

Corbin, Kentucky, mission trip 2005

Read Matthew 11:15. Yes, you have probably heard this before. Jesus often said it. In NIV, it reads, "He who has ears, let him hear." Upon hearing this in the past, you may have thought, "Well, we all have ears, so why did he even say that?" But I think that the New Living

Translation spells out what Jesus really meant. It says, "Anyone who is willing to hear should listen and understand!"

Are you willing to hear what God is saying to you? Will you try to listen and understand? These are questions that you should ask yourself every moment of your life, and the answer should be "Yes." While I realize that we all have our dry spells and off-days, you should always be ready for a message from God, because you never know when he will show up and speak.

"MILK" DEVOTIONS • 2003

I hope when my two boys are teenagers that they will love our God the way BJ did. The journal entries of BJ's gave me such an understanding of how the Lord can use our children to touch the lives of others. I want my boys to long after God the way BJ did.... and yes, when my boys experience the call to go, like BJ did, I will let them go—because of BJ's testimony.

KRISTINA • WILMORE, KENTUCKY
BLOG POSTING • SEPTEMBER 26, 2005

BJ's life and death changed our youth group, and it changed our church. God obviously used the prayers of a few friends and me who were praying the same thing. We were just praying for a revolution. BJ wanted that. He talked about it a lot.

JACK MEILS

[At the same time as] my heart is grieved at writing this to you, your son is being rewarded with a crown of life. Jim Elliot, a missionary in South America in the 1950s, is quoted as saying, "Lord, I don't ask for a long life, but a full one like yours, Lord Jesus." BJ had a full life. I predict that God will use this event to change the hearts of our country's youth in the same way Jim Elliot's death on the mission field did.

BILLY COLLIER • NEWCASTLE, OKLAHOMA
BLOG POSTING • SEPTEMBER 26, 2005

One heart touched by BJ's story was that of Bart Millard, lead singer of MercyMe. During much of BJ's final battle, Bart and the band were in upstate New York recording their album *Coming Up to Breathe*. They joined the ranks of the thousands who found themselves inexplicably drawn to the blog site, reading daily and praying through each new challenge.

Bart's conversation with Dad while BJ lay fighting, in fact, helped inspire the writing of the song "Bring the Rain." Its lyrics express a surrender to anything that brings God glory. BJ would have certainly approved.

God has really challenged me (and my teammates) over this Peru trip always to OBEY him immediately, to FOLLOW him with faith and endurance, and to SEEK after him and his glory.

WWW.XANGA.COM/DEADSILENCE7 • JULY 25, 2005

That kind of catapulted "Bring the Rain" into action—everything we'd been going through, and that conversation with Brent and his attitude through the blog site. Just, "If this is the way it's supposed to be, then we're in—we just want God's will to happen." It's nearly impossible to hear a dad say that, knowing it's his son whose life is on the line. It was pretty inspiring for those of us watching from the outside.

BART MILLARD

BJ's death hit Bart especially hard. He remembers running and playing with a five-year-old BJ at Northside just before a weekend youth event. Not long before BJ's death, Bart had watched and prayed at the hospital bedside of his own son. He had also lost several loved ones to death within the previous year.

It was while we were in the studio that BJ passed away. I remember that morning, just a few days before, it was like,

"He's made a big turn; it looks like he's maybe okay; we think we're going to make it." Then that one morning, the post was just really short: "At (whatever time that morning) BJ passed away."

I just kinda got the wind knocked out of me—I didn't see that one coming at all. It was a pretty down day in the studio.

BART MILLARD

Early in October Dad's brother Brad traveled with Rusty Kennedy and others to help in the cleanup after Hurricane Katrina. At the time, Bart was working to add lyrics to some music that MercyMe had held on to for a while. He began communicating with his friend Rusty via text messages, telling him about one more avenue for BJ's story: the song that became "I Would Die for You."

It was as though he was writing it as we texted back and forth. I told him, "If you're going to write a song about BJ, there's no way you can soft sell the gospel. There's no way that BJ was about that." Bart was text messaging me the lines as he would write them. I showed it to Brad, not knowing what would come of it.

RUSTY KENNEDY

Rusty mentioned to him that to accurately portray BJ, the song had to directly point others toward Christ. Bart's response was, "Don't worry."

UNCLE BRAD • BLOG POSTING • JUNE 24, 2006

Band members quickly laid down tracks for the song—the only one that every one of them agreed should make the cut for the album. Later, the London Sessions Orchestra would add background strings to the album, including a haunting cello line at the end of "I Would Die for You."

> There is no way that anyone in MercyMe could have known that BJ played the cello. That was such a "God thing" and makes the song even more special.
>
> Mom

Sometime in November, Rusty invited us, along with Lauren and Whitney, over to a friend's house, where we listened to a demo version of "I Would Die for You" set to a video featuring pictures from BJ's life. Until that night we had no idea that the song even existed. Our family, and the Northside family who heard the song a few weeks later, was amazed at the way God used Bart to communicate BJ's message.

> *John 15:13: The greatest love, the greatest way to love and obey Christ is to lay down your life for him: A) to lay down your sense of self and follow and obey him in living; B) to die for him.*
>
> PERU JOURNAL • JULY 3, 2005

> Bart called while they were listening to it and talked to them for about fifteen or twenty minutes. He explained why they wrote the song and that all the proceeds were going to go for missionaries to take BJ's place. It was a pretty exciting night for us all.
>
> RUSTY KENNEDY

> The song fully described what BJ did: he died for him—there was no other way to put it. He was willing to do whatever God wanted.
>
> TAYLOR DEBAUN

Whitney, BJ, and Lauren

> We listened to the song, and Bart was on the phone while the song was played for us. It was a very moving time, and we were overwhelmed. After we got off the phone, Rusty said something to us: "I think this is the first in a long line of this kind of thing that's going to happen as the result of your son."
>
> Dad

A lot of things I read that Brent posted on the blog site that BJ had written in his journal, a lot of that stuff kind of came out in these lyrics. You know, it's not really a song about BJ, so to speak. I guess you could say it was inspired by him. It's really a prayer that, hopefully, all of us can somehow get to a point where we can live it or at least confess that and say, "I would die for you."

There is a possibility that this life isn't going to just be a bed of roses from here on out. Are we willing to make a sacrifice for the kingdom? Because that's what BJ did. You can call it some weird disease or whatever, but he was on the mission field, and he was doing more than most forty- to fifty-year-olds have done in their entire lives.

I think that something spiritual did take place. There were a lot of [evil] powers-that-be that didn't want BJ doing what he was doing. I just think something much bigger than this took place in BJ's life and in his death. Reading the blog and just kind of going through it with them, even from a distance, you start looking at your own life and realizing how insignificant it really is. I may die of old age in my sleep and [my life would] not have as much meaning as BJ's life did.

So "I Would Die for You" is a challenge, a battle cry for all the body.

Bart Millard

Bart had seen the second story and was sharing it with the world. "Dying daily," surrendering to Christ in every area of life, was the message of BJ Higgins. The message of "I Would Die for You."

It's not a matter of what I want to do with my life, because if you are a true Christian, it's not even your life that you are living. Part of becoming a Christian is SURRENDERING your life to Christ. The Bible says "For I have been crucified with Christ; I no longer live, but Christ lives within me."

HTTP://THENO1HANGOUT.PROBOARDS3.COM • MAY 6, 2004

BJ's life is a picture to me of how we're supposed to do it. I was talking to Tara Case [another member of the Peru 2005 team], and she told me that we cannot allow BJ to be the exception. He has to be the rule. This stuck with me for a long time. The way he lived his life wasn't supposed to be extraordinary. BJ cannot be the exception. He has to be the rule.

KRISTIN DUTT • PERU 2005

All those who knew BJ agree that the only reason he might have ever agreed to a book about his life would be if he knew that, like the MercyMe song, his story would point directly to Jesus. BJ would also invite you to see the second story, to look with your heart, to discover how God is calling *you* to take his place. It may not be as a martyr, maybe not even as someone who serves as a missionary in the traditional sense. However, God does ask you to give up your time—your desires—your self—your life—to be willing to respond to whatever he says with a heartbeat of obedience.

It's time that we as the professed Christians of America wake up from our sleep of lethargy and hypocrisy and stop only living for Christ on Sundays and Wednesdays and start acting as Christ says all of his disciples must act. (As Luke 14:27 says, "Whoever

210

does not bear his own cross and come after me CANNOT be my disciple.")

We must die to ourselves daily. We must forget our comfort zones and our cliques of friends and go out and share the love and rescuing truth of Jesus Christ with the lost, empty, suffering, and dying people of the world all around us as Christ commanded!

Our lives are for Christ, not ourselves, so as it instructs in Hebrews 12:1–3, we need to actively, forcefully, and even violently (spiritually speaking) THROW off everything that hinders glorifying Christ through our lives! Don't want to because you enjoy your life? But Christ says "I have come that they may have life, and that they may have it more abundantly" (John 10:10b). You see, because we were made to glorify God, it is the one thing that satisfies us most and that we can find the most enjoyment in. We spend our lives seeking satisfaction and enjoyment, but it's only to be found in Christ. So what better reason to turn to him and let go and throw off everything that holds you back?

www.xanga.com/DeadSilence7 • August 2, 2005

BJ was ready to suffer and die physically because he had embraced a life of suffering, of "daily Christian dying" to self and selfish desires. He understood what was truly important. He knew what he would die for.

Do you?

I Would Die for You

And I know that I can find You here
'Cause You promised me You'll always be there
Times like these it's hard to see
But somehow I have a peace You're near

And I pray that You will use my life
In whatever way Your name is glorified
Even if surrendering means leaving everything behind

211

Chorus:
And my life has never been this clear
Now I know the reason why I'm here
You never know why you're alive
Until you know what you would die for . . .
I would die for You.

And I know I don't have much to give
But I promise You I'll give You all there is.
Can I possibly do less
When through Your own death I live?

(Chorus)

No greater love is found
Than of those who lay their own lives down
As sure as I live and breathe
Now I know what it means to be free

(Chorus)

Hallelujah. I would die for You. *(repeats)*

Taking BJ's Place
North Africa

In 2005 BJ returned from Peru with a powerful call on his heart, a call to North Africa. Once again, he planned to serve with Awe Star Ministries. His team would travel to a country where it is illegal for its citizens to invite Christ into their lives. They would build relationships and watch for God-given opportunities. More than fifty years before, Grandpa Higgins, finishing his term in the Air Force, had spent time in this same part of the world, in the city where BJ's journey would begin.

Even before returning from Peru, BJ excitedly shared his call to North Africa with us during a brief phone call. When he got home, everyone who talked to him heard about "next summer" when he would travel to North Africa.

Quickly God verified our son's call through our prayers. Before long, BJ entered the hospital. Soon, we envisioned that he would have a new testimony to take to North Africa. He would tell of the One who raised him from suffering to service.

The situation changed, but the testimony remained the same. In April 2006, after months of prayer on all sides, Dad joined the Awe Star staff as vice president for international operations.

That June the two of us helped lead a mission team of nineteen, including both Lauren and Whitney. Our destination was the same North African country to which God had called our son and brother.

Some of those who joined our journey were BJ's former teammates. Others had committed themselves at his memorial calling. All were committed to take his place.

On our first day in country, team members and several companions drove as far as vehicles could safely travel and then hiked to the nearby mountains. Here, amid tall pines and towering peaks,

Our family at BJ's cairn, high above North Africa

we held a final memorial service. Here we laid the remains of our young warrior's earthly body to rest.

Prayerfully each one shared a Scripture and other words. Each one laid a river stone over the humble site.

BJ's body had reached the country for which his heart yearned. BJ's team carried out the calling he had been unable to

complete. BJ's legacy continues—in Peru, in North Africa, and beyond.

It's time to raise a revolution. God will give you the strength.

Site of BJ's ashes

IM Conversation
Zach's Salvation through BJ's Witness

Zach: so wat have u been up 2

Zach: hey bj

BJ: hey

BJ: well, i just got back from a 5 week trip to Peru

Zach: oh kool

Zach: hey i have something 2 tell u

Zach: that i think u will like it

BJ: cool

Zach: ok

Zach: i want 2 give my life 2 christ

Zach: but how

BJ: When Jesus called his disciples, he said "come and follow me." he made it clear that all we need to do is to simply believe in him and FOLLOW him and obey him.

Zach: ok

BJ: Giving your life to Christ is a simple matter of surrendering. Just simply praying and saying that you give your wants, dreams, ambitions, comforts, and goals to Christ because you realize that you can't make it on your own

Zach: yes i want 2 do that

BJ: In the Bible, Christ talks about how he gives us joy and a new chance to make things right if we would just live for him

BJ: all you have to do is pray

Zach: ok i want 2 be a follower of god

BJ: Jesus said we can talk straight to God because of him, so just tell God: God I know that I've done many wrong things and that that separates me from you, but I believe that you loved me so much that you sent your Son, Jesus Christ to die for me, then raised him from the dead so that I can have eternal life and freedom from sin and victory over death. God I want to have a personal relationship with you and follow you. I want you to be the master over my life.

BJ: An important thing to following Christ is knowing where he's going, which is known through reading the Bible, praying and spending time with other people who have the same relationship with Jesus Christ and also follow him, which can be done through going to church. God also wants us to sing about, worship, and glorify him, which can be done through singing songs to God

Zach: yes that's what i want

BJ: And if you pray that prayer, and truly mean it, the Bible says that he will never leave you, that he will always be with you and give you strength and joy.

BJ: Then pray. The words aren't magic or important by themselves, but if you really mean it, the Bible says that God will save you. Pray: "God I know that I've done many wrong things and that that separates me from you, but I believe that you loved me so much that you sent your Son, Jesus Christ to die for me, then raised him from the dead so that I can have eternal life and freedom from sin and victory over death. God I want to have a personal relationship with you and follow you. I want you to be the master over my life."

Zach: ok i did

BJ: awesome! That means that you are now my brother in Christ!

Zach: yes sweet

Zach: and i really did mean it 2

BJ: awesome, man! Well, I really encourage you to get plugged in at a church so that you can grow with Christ, and not just stay in the same place. Of course, its not about traditions or religion, but God gave us the church as a means of meeting with other believers and worshipping and growing in him

Zach: i have one

BJ: awesome, which is it?

Zach: but it's _____ and i do sometimes go 2 ur old church

BJ: ok, well I know that my old church is pretty solid . . . unfortunately, there are a lot of churches out there that say that they follow Jesus, but they are actually fake, so its hard to sift through and find one that is for real, but they're out there.

BJ: Also, as far as reading the Bible, I encourage you to start reading a little bit every day, so that you can get to know God better, and what he wants you to do with your new life.

BJ: I would start in the book of John

BJ: There is some really powerful stuff in there.

Zach: ok then what

BJ: Also, if you ever have any questions, just gimme an email or a call

Zach: what is ur email

BJ: God also wants us to make a habit of talking to him everyday (after all, it's not much of a relationship if we don't talk). It doesn't matter where you are or what you're doing, you can talk to God and ask him to help you or just thank him for what he's done

BJ: [gives address and address of xanga weblog]

BJ: also, I know I said a lot of stuff in this convo, and so its easy to miss some, but if you want, i'd save the convo, and then check the things I said with what you read in John and the rest of the Bible. But I believe you'll find it to be accurate

Zach: ok hey i know this is gonna sound stupid but how do u hear god answer ur prayers

Zach: and how do u start a prayer

Zach: and how do u know wat 2 tell him

BJ: Well, I've found that God answers prayer through several ways, sometimes he speaks through other Christians (not to say everything they say is from God, but he does use them), through circumstances, but mostly through the Bible

BJ: To start a prayer, you just start it like you would any conversation, call him by name. For example "Dad, i just want to thank you for the great things you've given me, but I just ask that you help me and give me strength because I'm really struggling with this thing . . ."

BJ: but our prayers don't have to be exact or fit into one pattern. God just wants us to talk to him and ask him for help, thank him for things he gives us, or just tell him what's on our minds.

Zach: ok

Zach: but here's what i have trouble w/

BJ: If one day you really feel like you need to know how to do something, like how to treat someone or respond to a situation, just ask God to help, but ask earnestly, believing that he'll answer, and really seek him on it, or keep on asking, and he'll give you what you need.

Zach: ok here's my thing

Zach: How do u know that he is "Answering ur prayers"

BJ: For instance, if you pray and ask God to help you get through something, like a hard relationship, or a sickness, or just a crappy day. God may answer your prayer by just giving you energy, or helping you to be nice, or just giving you more courage to press on. God answers prayer in all kinds of ways. Through other people sometimes. You may pray that God would give you wisdom, then someone gives you advice, or you just "figure out" what to do. God works through nature and through other things a lot. There are no coincidences. Everything in our lives, God orchestrates. So if one random event helps you get through a day, or if someone you prayed for gets better, that's not a coincidence or just something cool that happened to match up with your prayers, that is God working and answering your prayers

BJ: But i can't really describe it to you. I just challenge you to pray, and like it says in James 1, to pray with faith, and really believe that what you pray will be answered and that God knows what is best for you (even though it's not always what we want at that moment).

BJ: To find out how God answers prayers, pray and see what happens, but don't get discouraged if it feels like you aren't being answered right away. God is in control of each situation, but sometimes he

waits to answer or allows us to go through a hardship so that we
can become stronger and rely more and more on him

Zach: ok i think i get is

Zach: it

Zach: a li

Zach: lil

BJ: those are all good questions you are asking. Sometimes we don't get
it all right away. God is really deep and we'll never get it completely,
but he just asks that we seek to get as much as possible.

Zach: dude thanx soooo much

BJ: So I would start by reading the book of John, about a chapter a
day, and really thinking about what it says. It's confusing at times
(especially if you have certain translations of the Bible like King
James Version), but that's when you pray that God would help you
to understand

BJ: it's my pleasure, man:-D

BJ: i'm so excited that you came to me about this!

BJ: You can now say, without a doubt, that you are going to heaven
and that you will be my brother forever because you follow Christ,
who is the purpose and meaning of life!!

Zach: yep i am 2

BJ: :-D

Zach: i will c u up there along w/ taylor and lots of other ppl

BJ: you will:-)

BJ: remember, if you ever have any other questions, go to God first,
but feel free to ask me as well, and i can try to answer them as best
I can

Zach: ok thanx sooo much

BJ: your so welcome

BJ: well, if you don't have any other questions, i gotta go to bed pretty
soon. I'll be praying for you

Zach: i will be prayin now

BJ: for you, that God would continue to show himself to you and
teach you.

BJ: awesome

Zach: yes

Zach: i will pray 4 u

BJ: thank you

Zach: yep

Zach: later

Zach: u need 2 get on line more and we can talk

Zach: do u check ur email alot

BJ: yeah

BJ: i'm on email a lot more than aim

Zach: ok

BJ: but i'll try to get on aim more

Zach: ok

Zach: thanx man sooo much 4 wat u did 4 me just then

Zach: and also want 2 thank u 4 being the person helpin me out here

Zach: w// all of this stuff

BJ: oh dude, i did nothing, this is an example of how God works: God spoke through me and saved you, and I'm just praisin him for doin it! But I do try to do my part to be obedient and let him speak, but like I said, it's been my pleasure

BJ: :-D well goodnight, brother

Zach: yea later

Zach: bi

Zach: thanx bi

Frequently Asked Questions

How can I give?

BJ's Hope is a privately endowed scholarship fund created to honor the memory of BJ Higgins. The scholarship will allow students who share his passion for the lost to take BJ's place in taking the gospel to the nations. For more information or to apply for the scholarship, check out BJ's Hope at www.awestar.org.

Tax-deductible contributions toward this fund may be sent to:

> BJ's Hope Scholarship Fund
> c/o Awe Star Ministries
> P.O. Box 470265
> Tulsa, OK 74147-0265

How can I go?

Is God calling you to take BJ's place on the mission field? Check out the possibilities available through Awe Star Ministries (BJ's sending organization) at www.awestar.org. You'll find opportunities intentionally designed to equip you for serving others across the world.

Frequently Asked Questions

Contact Awe Star at info@awestar.org; 1-800-AweStar; or Awe Star Ministries, P.O. Box 470265, Tulsa, OK 74147-0265.

Who are these people, anyway?

Brent Higgins (Dad), an ordained minister and popular speaker, has worked with students for more than fifteen years. He is a graduate of Purdue University and serves as the vice president for international operations of Awe Star Ministries in Tulsa, Oklahoma. Awe Star networks with thousands of churches worldwide, providing students with opportunities to take BJ's place through global missions. Brent and his wife, Deanna, are loving parents of Lauren, Whitney, and BJ.

Deanna Higgins (Mom), an accomplished singer, musician, and music teacher, is a graduate of Houston Baptist University. She especially enjoys serving alongside her husband, helping lead teams of students overseas, and sharing in song as he speaks in churches across the world.

How can I learn more or invite Brent and Deanna Higgins to share at my church, school, or other group?

Blog Site: www.prayforbj.com (daily posts; pictures and videos of BJ; important links)

Email: brent.higgins@awestar.org

1-800-AweStar
Brent and Deanna Higgins
c/o Awe Star Ministries
P.O. Box 470265
Tulsa, OK 74147-0265

Acknowledgments

Above all, we would like to thank our Lord and Savior, Jesus Christ. Without him, there would be no testimony to share, and this work would be only an inspirational story rather than a battle cry.

So many people contributed to the process of growing our son into a warrior for Christ. Please allow us to focus on a few who had an especially significant impact on his spiritual development. In order of appearance in his life, we would like to thank his sisters Lauren and Whitney, Gramma and Grandpa Higgins, Mamaw and Papaw Tucker, Uncle Brad, Uncle Rich, Mrs. Dailey, Rusty, Big John, David, Walker, Philip, Tito, and Larry.

Thank you to our extended families who contributed significantly through prayer, visits, and encouragement. Thank you, Dan and Stephen, for your work on our home while Beej was hospitalized.

We would like to thank our dear friends who stood with us through this journey. We already knew you as our friends, but your lives in Christ shone with great radiance through the six-week hospital stay. Big John and Jeannie, Lowell and Carol, Rusty and Michelle (thank you for the blog site), Larry and Brenda, Glen and Gabe, Jim (thank you for the DVDs), Bill and Karen,

Acknowledgments

Janice, our small group, and finally, Brad (thank you for staying with us every day and through the watches of the night).

St. Vincent's Children's Hospital PICU staff, you have blessed us with your heroic efforts and unceasing care. We will never forget you.

Thanks to Northside Baptist Church, Crosswinds Community Church, First Baptist Church of Mooresville, Awe Star Ministries, and the thousands of bloggers who offered us unwavering prayer support and encouragement. Danny and Jeff, the blog would never have been possible without your gifts and expertise. Thank you again.

Thanks to MercyMe for your friendship, your ministry, and a song that continues to touch hearts across the world. Thanks for setting up the endowment for BJ's Hope Missions Scholarship Fund. Thank you, Bart, for taking the time to speak with us (first with our family and again for this book) about "I Would Die for You."

Thanks to Billy and Cindy Foote for your friendship, for ministering at BJ's memorial celebration, and for leading us to the throne through your writing, music, and example.

Thank you, family, along with BJ's friends, mentors, fellow missionaries, and caregivers, for contributing words, time, and especially prayers in the preparation of this work. Your stories continue to bless and comfort us. Thanks to Chris Ferebee for believing in this story and assisting us in taking BJ's message to the world.

Thank you, Marti, for listening during hundreds of hours of conversation, interviews, and discussion. Thank you for your tireless efforts, sensitive spirit, and intercession on this most personal project.

Thanks especially to all those who find inspiration in BJ's testimony. We are praying for you as you take his place in raising a revolution.